SAY GOOD NIGHT,
Seymour

Roberta Ferguson Trail

This book is dedicated to Ray, my soulmate and husband of more than fifty years, and to Ray, Mark, and Mike, our three sons, who made us proud every day. We all learned that anyone can accomplish anything by working hard and never giving up.

POLTERGEIST

A GERMAN WORD MEANING A NOISY
USUALLY MISCHIEVOUS GHOST

ACKNOWLEDGMENTS

I would like to thank my daughter-in-law, Lisa Trail, who has the patience of a saint. I am not tech savy and she helped me with my computer and was always redoing my files. Lisa was in the process of editing my manuscript when she gave a draft copy to her sister, Linda Busz, to read. Linda shared this copy with two of her friends, Tom Graham and Edna Cino. Together they read every page. Their notes and kind words of encouragement gave me the confidence to submit my work to a publisher. They were my first fans so I owe them a special debt of thanks.

I would also like to thank Kathleen Zingaro Clark, a published author who encouraged my writing from the very beginning. A special thanks goes to my Florida neighbor and friend, Maureen Dombrowski, former newspaper copy editor and English teacher, who helped me polish the final drafts of my manuscript.

Finally, I would like to express my gratitude for a chance meeting with the famous writer, Martha Grimes. She is a gracious, talented woman who came to visit me on our farm when it was under contract. Our realtor had just sold her a farm in Bucks County, Pa, and thought we might have some antiques to sell. Although we had no antiques that we wanted to part with, Ms. Grimes enjoyed seeing our animals and hearing their stories. Her mystery novels often include animal stories since she is a passionate animal lover and a strong advocate for animal welfare as am I. We talked over a cup of tea, and she told me anyone can write if they have a story to tell. Well, I am about to find out.

My thanks to everyone.

CHAPTER ONE

The house is quiet as I stand here alone in what was once my living room. It is a strange feeling of loneliness. Today my house belongs to someone else.

How did this happen? I had expected to grow old here and be buried out in the pastures with my horses when they passed away.

I can hear voices overhead. The new owners are upstairs, going through my home one room at a time, led by my husband and the realtors. Everyone sounds excited. Everyone has reason to be happy. The real estate agency has just been paid a big commission check. We have been paid a large sum of money for all our years of hard work and restoration. The new owners have just purchased a beautiful 268-year-old Pennsylvania stone farmhouse on fifteen acres. Yet here I stand alone and brooding.

My sense of loss is real. I love this place. There are so many things about the farm I am going to miss, but most of all, I will miss you, Seymour; I am very sure you will be a big surprise to the new owners.

As I lean against the windowsill, my thoughts wander as I remember the first time I saw the farm house. Was it only thirteen years ago?

* * * * *

I was meeting a realtor at the property and had taken my two sons, Mark and Mike, along for the ride. I pulled up a gravel driveway and into a courtyard, continued around the circle, and came to a stop in front of a large stucco farmhouse.

My kids immediately began giving me their input—remarks like "Let's get out of here!" and "Where did you find this place?" There were even comments regarding my sanity. I tried to get them out of the car, to come with me, but they were like chewing gum on a carpet and impossible to remove.

Leaving them in the car, I walked up the flagstone walk to a screened-in porch and to the twin doors. As I looked around, I was beginning to agree with the boys. When I had spoken to the realtor sometime ago, I had told her I wanted an old farm, something that needed work but had the potential to be a beautiful estate.

After a quick look around, this definitely was not the place. The screened-in porch was torn and falling down. There were bags of trash piled helter-skelter just outside the door and the white stucco was streaked with rust. I could only assume the rust was coming from old rusted rain gutters. The stucco had not seen a coat of paint in some forty years.

Card that was given to us from the realtor.

This is the porch and the front of house when we bought the farmhouse.

This is the back of the house when we bought the
farm. This will later become the front of the house as
it would have been two hundred years ago.

Shows rust all over the stucco.

I knocked softly, ever so softly, and when no one answered, I breathed a sigh of relief and went quickly to my car and left. Back at home, I was not even in the door yet when I heard my phone ringing. It was the realtor begging me to come back and have a look at the property. She assured me that when I was inside, it would be everything I had been looking for and much more. So I drove back, leaving my little instigators behind.

I still cannot explain what it was that I fell in love with, but as the realtor opened up the door, I was standing in the dining room. Just to the right of me was a huge walk-in fireplace that took up the whole wall. I could feel the heat from the fire. The woman who owned the house was sitting by the fireplace in a rocker, a scene right out of *Currier & Ives*. Just to the left of the fireplace was a small door with a few steps that led into the kitchen. It was a small kitchen, and my mind was already at work.

I would knock out this wall and rip out the cabinets. Then the realtor interrupted my planning and took my arm, leading me back through the dining room. We walked into a hallway, and I could now see where the twin doors had been on the porch. One door led into the dining room, and one led into the main hallway, where I saw a staircase. The realtor rolled back tall drawing-room doors to a very large living room. To the left of me were built-in bookcases, and straight in front of me was a stone fireplace.

The hardwood floors were not the original, and I already knew they would have to be replaced. The dining room and living room were large rooms with deep windowsills. I was falling in love with what I saw. When we walked through the living room and through another door into an L-shaped wing, straight in front of me was another staircase.

"Just how many staircases are there?" I asked the realtor.

"Three," she answered. "One at each end of the house and the one in the center hall we just passed."

A powder room was just beyond the staircase. We turned back past the staircase and went down a short hall to the library.

We stepped down into a large room with fourteen-foot ceilings, and to my right was a large window, almost the size of the wall with a black marble sill just a few feet off the floor. The view from the picture window overlooked the fields, and I was looking back at the original farmhouse. I was amazed at the size of the house.

I turned back into the room, and there was a corner fireplace from ceiling to floor, all in raised panel, painted in colonial green. It was a very impressive room. Surrounding the fireplace opening were Mercer tiles. The realtor explained that each tile told the story of a harvest. The prestigious Mercer Tile Museum and tile works were not far away in Doylestown. The hearth was black marble and matched the marble on the windowsill. When I looked behind me, there were built-in bookcases. Someone had spent a great deal of money on this L-shaped addition.

The realtor explained that in the 1940s, the house was owned by a very prominent family who owned department stores in the area. They had indeed spared no expense in building this L-shaped wing onto the end of this very old farmhouse.

The realtor did not know the age of the farmhouse but thought it might date back to the 1700s. We left the library and went up the staircase, still in this addition, to the second floor and the second-floor master suite. This was as surprising as the library.

The bedroom was a large room with a fireplace and four windows with deeps sills with paned glass. If I had not been wearing those glasses, the rose-colored ones, then I might have noticed the wallpaper sliding off the walls and the paint curled up on the windowsill under a hundred years of paint throughout the rest of the house.

Or perhaps I missed the missing panes of glass in the window that had been shot out and the rugs throughout the home that were so badly stained you would need protective gear to tear them out.

No, I was looking only at what I wanted to see. The realtor had noticed that I had stopped my oohs and aahs, and she said, "It only needs a little TLC. A coat of paint would do wonders. You did say you didn't mind some hard work, didn't you?"

She was right. I had said I was looking for a fixer-upper.

We continued down a hallway lined with closets and into a dressing room. Just off the dressing room was the master bathroom. It had a tub and separate stall shower; even the ceiling was tiled in the shower that had a glass door. This was state of the art for a bathroom built in the 1940s. A paned glass window looked out over the circle I had just pulled around. A huge mirror and vanity completed the master bath.

Back through the bedroom and down the short hallway, we turned into the original farmhouse. We were now in the early part of the house. This would have been the master bedroom. In the days before funeral homes, it would have been the room that was used to lay out the deceased family member. I'd have to make sure this was never mentioned to my sons as this might be one of their bedrooms.

From this bedroom, we entered another hallway. On the left, there was a small bathroom with a claw-foot tub. Everywhere you looked, there were windows with lots of light. In retrospect, I should have been looking down more at my feet, at the flooring beneath them that would have to be replaced—the tile floors, hardwood floors, and carpets.

But I was enchanted.

Down the hall on the right was the next bedroom. It was small and, at one time, had been a little girl's room. There was a vanity that was built in the corner of the room. Even this room had two large windows. Just as we left this room, there was another set of stairs that led to the third floor. It was a short set of steps to a landing and turned to another short set of steps to the top. I would not know for some time that this stairway was built over the original butterfly steps from two hundred years ago.

The term *butterfly steps* is used for the steps one finds in old farmhouses that start out from a corner of just a few inches and get wider as they go to the wall. It would be one of many things I was going to learn about this farmhouse.

The third floor was another surprise. Someone had renovated the top of the house and put a large wall of windows, starting from the original window dormer to the other dormer. It created a wall of windows. Just to the left of this was another bathroom.

It was then that I asked, "Just how many bathrooms are there in this house?"

She answered, "There are four full baths on the second floor, including this one on the third floor, and two powder rooms on the first floor, one at each end of the house."

I was just now beginning to think of who was going to clean all of them. At the end of the bath was a door that led to what was left of the original attic. It still had the original flooring, and as I looked ahead, I could see the opening that led to the crawl space over the rooms. A chill went through me, but it was winter so I ignored it, thinking it just a draft. We continued on.

We left the third floor. Back in the hallway, we made a short turn, and there on the right was the center staircase. We had made it to the halfway point of the center of the house. I was beginning to understand the layout of the home as I had been lost up to this point. We continued down a short hallway with windows on my left and a hall bathroom on the right. It was a large room with a tub, a small sink, and a toilet. It needed a total rehab. My ideas were larger than my pocketbook.

This was one of the four bathrooms the realtor had told me about. The hall bath was adjacent to another bedroom. Again it was another light-filled bedroom with built-in bookcases at one end. On the other side was an alcove with three windows arched around in a semicircle. All these bedrooms that I had just looked at had fireplaces in each one but had been closed off and plastered over. This had been a practical thing to do at the turn of the century. Now that there were heated homes, they did not require to heat with only fireplaces.

The realtor had just pointed this out to me, showing me where the fireplace would have been in this room. There were seven fireplaces in all, and I wondered how anyone could keep seven fireplaces burning at one time. That would have been a full-time job.

In the middle of the room were two steps down into the last room at the end of the house. It was a small room again with three very large windows.

The plaster was peeling off the ceiling and all around the windows. I could not be sure if it was the roof leaking, the windows leaking, or both.

By now I had fallen into silence. All the floors would have to be replaced upstairs and downstairs, carpets needed to be replaced in all the bedrooms, and possibly a new roof—oh and a new kitchen. And did I mention new bathrooms?

The realtor was looking at me deep in thought and, as if she could read my mind, said, "Not everything has to be done right away."

We left the second floor, walking down the butterfly steps, and came into the kitchen. This was the third staircase and must be originally at the end of the house. A door in the kitchen led to the basement. I would leave that to my husband to look at. He could inspect the furnace, water heaters, plumbing, wiring, etc. That was his forte, and I would not know what I was looking at. I made another appointment for my husband to see the house.

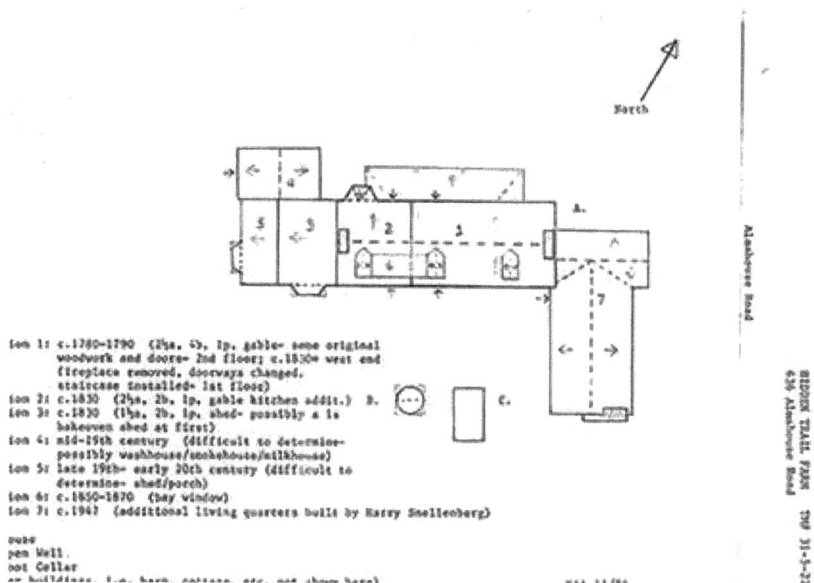

This drawing was done by the Bucks County Conservancy on a visit in May 1984. It shows the many expansions over the years. Item #5 was the addition completed by the Trail family.

CHAPTER TWO

I drove home excited. We had been looking for a farm for a lot of reasons. We needed a shop for my husband's business, and I needed a barn for my horse, a palomino quarter horse named Dusty. She had been a gift from my husband for my twenty-eighth birthday, and I had been boarding her for the last five years. I loved horses and dreamed of owning a farm one day. My boys all wanted ground to ride their own three-wheelers. Only my oldest son already had one. He was in trouble with the neighbors every time he started to ride as it broke the silence of our quiet suburban neighborhood. We all had reasons to want to buy a place with a lot of ground and no neighbors.

We were very friendly with our neighbors, and we wanted it to stay that way. Sadly, we had outgrown our present home. We had found this home eleven years ago all boarded up in a very beautiful area of Huntingdon Valley. The builder had just stopped working on the home, and we bought the house from him on a handshake. He was an older man from Scotland and believed that your word was as good as your handshake.

When I asked if we needed a lawyer, he answered, "Can you read?"

"Of course," I said.

"Then why would you need a lawyer?" he answered.

It had no bathrooms or kitchen. There were no steps or windows. Boards covered where the windows should have been. We had agreed on a price, and we would have two years at our expense to finish the house as we liked. We had agreed on a price and would only pay interest on the price agreed upon. The interest was to be paid every six months. It turned out to be a very good deal, and it was to be our first home renovation. When we had completed our agreement two years later and had finished the house, we thought we were experienced builders.

Oh, did we have a lot to learn!

Ray and I had married young. We did not have the best of childhoods and believed we could have a better life together. We both had strong work ethics and good jobs. We would pass this on to our boys. They were taught to mow the lawn, keep their rooms clean, and help their dad around the house with any projects.

Ray had started his own business at twenty-eight years old. We had already been married for ten years and had three boys. He had been employed in a steel foundry, and they had paid for his college education. He went for industrial electricity and would work for this mill for ten years. He left there on very good terms, and the steel mill would be one of his very first customers. Life had been good up until now.

The farmhouse was being sold *as is* and needed a lot of work. I hadn't looked at the barn or the little guesthouse or the pool area. I would see this all with my husband.

I knew Ray would bring me back to reality when I got home.

It had taken about a year before I could talk him into doing our first renovation on our present home. I was quite sure he would never agree to this farmhouse. We would be looking at years before we could make this place our home—not to mention the days and nights of no sleep, just work. Although we were willing to do all the labor, we would still need money for dumpsters, materials, appliances, flooring, etc. It had taken all of two years to finish our present home, and this house could fit in one end of this farmhouse or be lost completely in the barn.

Oh, what was I thinking!

Ray and I had just finished looking at the farmhouse. I was shocked he still wanted to see the rest of the property. The barn was twelve thousand square feet and was L-shaped like the house. When we opened up the barn doors, there were old makeshift stalls. It would need to be cleaned up as it had been a warehouse for other people's junk. We took the steps up to the second floor. I was overwhelmed with the sheer amount of items that people had left behind. No one who had ever moved from here went to a bigger home, so everything they didn't want was left here.

The biggest surprise was just ahead of us. We threaded our way around old dishwashers and boxes of other people's discards when we came to a door that led into the wing of the barn.

From behind us we heard the realtor say, "Be careful. There is no floor out there!"

We opened the door to see timbers and flooring that had collapsed. Each floor had fallen onto the next. The roof had caved in, and all three floors had collapsed from the rain and snow. When we looked up, we were looking out at the sky. Just in front of us were timbers, old roof singles, and soggy plywood. This disaster had been years in the making. The whole wing was ready for the dumpster.

The small guesthouse was painted in many colors but held promise. There was a fireplace in a living room, and to the right was a small kitchenette. In the bathroom was a stall shower and sink. We found a small plaque that told us this was a Sears and Roebucks prefab house. It was a complete home with a small bedroom. It was used as a pool house and just beyond the sliding doors and patio was a very large pool.

It came as no surprise to find a pool that would have to be completely removed. Instead of water, it was filled with drawings the largest of which was the sun. The cracks in the pool were wide enough to hide a body inside.

At one time in the 1940s and early '50s, this farm had been a beautiful estate. But from the time that the prominent family had sold the farm, it had started to decline. It would take a lifetime to restore this place, and I was already tired. We said our goodbyes to the realtor and walked to our car.

Ray had not said a word.

I asked, "Well, what do you think?"

He answered, "I like it."

CHAPTER THREE

---✦---

The farm had been on the market for three years with no offers. We had a lot of money in equity in our present home and believed we could handle this financially, so we made an offer. It was not even close to what they were expecting, so we came to our senses and walked away. We continued to look, but nothing we saw could compare to the ghost of what was once that estate. A year passed, and we had given up thinking about it.

One day I answered the phone to the realtor who had showed us the property. She said, "I am at the farmhouse you looked at last year." She went on to say that the owner was with someone making an offer on the farmhouse. It was the same offer we had made a year ago. The couple who was making the offer wanted the homeowner to remove all the trash from the property, and they wanted repairs to be made from a home inspection.

That was really funny!

It would require a core of army engineers and trailers of dumpsters, not to mention heavy equipment, just to clean up the place. We made an offer on the phone that day for the same price, but we would buy *as is* with no mortgage contingency and no inspections. This meant that upon our signature on the agreement of sale, we would have bought a farm. We would not for any reason be able to change our minds; it would be ours.

The realtor wanted to know if our offer was still good. We said, "Yes."

She was at the farm and presented the offer at that moment. That was how we bought the farm on that day. I never dreamed when I woke up that morning that, before nightfall, we would own a farm that would require a lifetime of work and money.

But we were young and fearless; we believed we could do the impossible. We had not yet sold our house and needed the equity in order to complete this purchase. The very first day we put our house up for sale, it sold. The only contingency—we move in thirty days. When I look back I am amazed at the chances we took. Sheer panic at where we would now live set in. We had expected to live here until the farm had been renovated. We couldn't believe our home had sold on the first day.

It would take three days for us to make a settlement on the farm. The woman who had owned the farm had taken rent on two horses that were being boarded there. The stalls were not safe for anyone's horses. I was not bringing Dusty up until the barn was cleaned out and finished. Some of the pasture fence was missing, and the pastures were so overgrown that a horse could be lost out there.

There was a lot of arguing, and we kept leaving the settlement table. Everyone was threatening to sue us. I could not blame the women who owned the farm. She was going through a divorce, and her husband had run off. She was dealing with three very difficult teenagers.

All I kept thinking was "There but for the grace of God go I."

I would not have wanted to be in her position. I suppose we had buyer's remorse, but there was no turning back now. We could not live in the farmhouse with the way it looked right now. We needed someplace to live. We talked about renting a trailer or buying one and then reselling it. The prices we were getting were out of the question. We needed every dollar for the house. We came up with the idea that we would renovate the pool house first. We could live in it for a few weeks. After all, it would only be a very short time.

I was wondering how I was going to break the news to our sons that they were now about to be enslaved along with their parents. Ray Jr. was just turning fourteen and was at an age to really give us his opinion. Mark, who was eleven years old, was also of strong character. I expected this would not be easy. Our youngest son, Michael, age seven, still believed that his parents were smart and knew what they were doing.

Just like their mom and dad, they too were caught up in their dreams of riding miles of fields and open spaces on their three-wheelers. We all had our dreams. But careful what you wish for; you could end up in a nightmare. Even our children fell under the spell of the farmhouse, or perhaps they just thought their parents had a lot of money.

We told them it was going to be an adventure. We said, "It will be a lot of hard work, but when we're finished, we will all have what we want."

Of course, the day I told them we were moving into a pool house did not go over so well.

It was the end of May, and they would soon be out of school so they would not have to tell any of their friends where they were moving until it was finished. At least, that was the plan! For the next thirty days, we packed and went to work while the boys went to school. In the evening, we all went to the farm and worked.

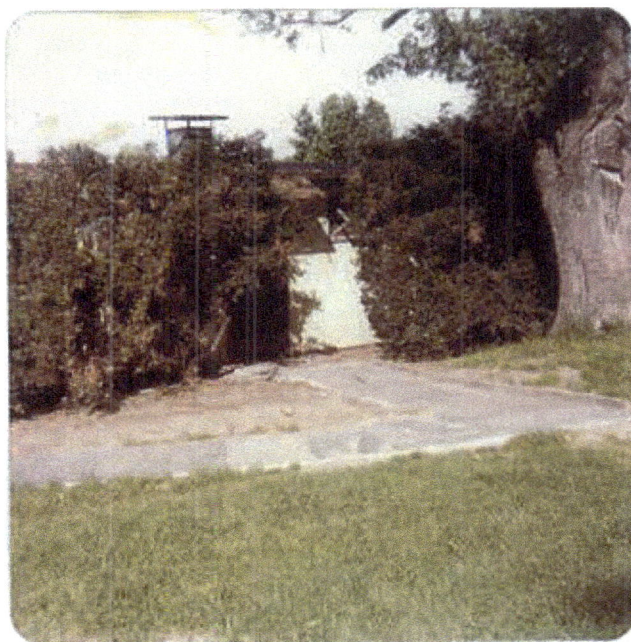

This was the pool house when the boys first saw it.

Chapter Four

I n the middle of all of this, we were coping with a very old boy who had been part of our lives for the past thirteen years. Young Ray was only a toddler when I had brought home a three-month old Doberman puppy. A very good friend of mine was working on a farm with show dogs. One of their females had puppies, and there was one puppy in particular that was not quite show quality. His ear was not standing up like it should.

He was an outcast. I liked him already when I heard this. His registered name was Stormsons Thunder Jet. I called him Jet. He was given to me as my friend knew he would have a home where he would be dearly loved. The first home we had purchased was a duplex apartment. It was our first investment. We lived in one apartment and collected rent on the other. Ray kept telling me we couldn't keep a dog in an apartment. He was not a big animal lover—not then anyway.

But he was in the hospital, having surgery on his shoulder. I was home alone, and it seemed a perfect time for me to have a puppy. After all, I was home raising a two-year-old, and one more baby would be no trouble. Ray came home from the hospital to find a dog sleeping in his bed. For the next thirteen years, Jet grew up with my children and was dearly loved by all of us.

I had had two operations done on his cancer, trying to cure him. We were trying to keep him with us as long as we could. But he was now in pain all the time. I knew in my heart it was time to let him go.

Why is it so hard to make that decision? You know it's the best that you can do for your companion, but getting the mind set to come to terms with the pain in your heart is something else. It's different for everyone when you have to make that decision to say good-bye. I swore I would never again do this to myself.

We were outside the vet's office, and I had told Ray we must stay there for him and held Jet so he would not know anything was wrong. But in the end, it was me who ran out of the office and Ray who stayed and held him in his arms. I was sitting in the car, sobbing, when Ray came out. He assured me that he had quietly gone to sleep. We sat there for the longest time while I sobbed. Ray sat quietly.

We were at the lowest point in our lives. We had just lost our companion, our best friend, and were going back to a farm that needed years of hard physical work and more money than we had. I had put my children in a pool house to live for an indefinite period of time. It felt like I had been hit with a Mack truck and run over. I had no way of knowing how long it would be until I felt some relief from my pain. Ray tried to console me, but he was grief-stricken as well.

Chapter Five

We now called it the "cottage" since it sounded so much better than "pool house." It was our primary focus. We had our first forty-yard dumpster on site and had filled it to the brim in less than a week with the junk from the second floor of the barn. This was where we were going to store all our furniture. Ray had brought up the company's backhoe, and we were making good time filling the bucket. Ray had taught young Ray how to operate it. He was our designated driver. He would pull up to the site to be cleared, and we would load the bucket. He would then drive over to the dumpster and raise the bucket and unload.

Mark, age 11, learning to operate the backhoe.

There was no such thing as too young. We had the largest dumpster you could get. We were filling them in a week. We would pack them so tight with the backhoe that, on a few occasions, the driver would come for the dumpster and have trouble picking them up.

We spent months cleaning up. There was the three-story wing of the barn that went into the dumpster. There was the trash that had been left in the barn on both floors. That included old bathtubs, sinks, and old appliances. Next was the kitchen that went into the dumpster. We took out everything that we would need to put into the dumpster. It would take a total of twenty-eight dumpsters before we were done with them, but it would take months before this happened.

The cottage, when first built, had been decorated like a ship, with two bunks attached on one side of the wall. A porthole was above each bunk and was a light. It was the same thing on the other side of the wall. There were four bunks in all, and this was part of the living room that held the fireplace. It was really a cute idea, and it would work well.

We painted over the colors of blue-and-yellow strips for a solid cream color. It was looking better already. I put twin fitted sheets on the bunks and covered them with cream-colored quilts and lots of throw pillows. It was late spring, so we bought a folding table and folding chairs in white lattice and put it on the patio. This was where we could have our meals on sunny days while looking at the painted sun on the pool. And on rainy days, we would bring our folding table and chairs into our living room and have our meals inside.

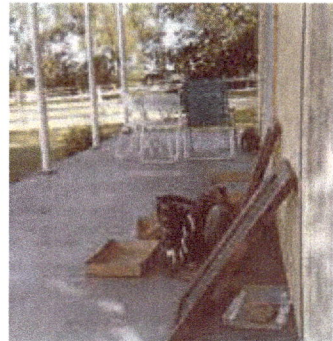

Our view from the back of the cottage where we ate each morning.

Our cottage now functioned as a dining room for meals either outdoor or indoor. In the evening, it would be our homework room and later our community bedroom. Ray Jr. and Mark slept in the top bunks, and Mike slept in the lower bunk. One bunk mattress was pulled on the floor for me. Ray slept on a portable mattress that during the day could be folded up and stored. It was very important that this small home be kept immaculate. It would be the only way I would keep my sanity.

The single bedroom was used as our dressing room, with poles holding our hanging clothes and chests of drawers housing everything else. We took turns getting dressed in the room each morning.

One day, little Mike's teacher sent home a note saying, "Your son was not prepared for school today as he did not have a pencil."

I took his note and wrote back on the same note, "We were lucky to find socks today, much less a pencil." I later learned they did not find that funny.

The cottage was looking good, complete with new carpeting and new kitchen cabinets, counters, and sink. We did not intend to be here very long, and one day we could use this once again as it had been intended—a pool house.

I awoke in the middle of the night and had to wake up Ray. I was having an anxiety attack. I couldn't breathe, and I was sure I was going to start screaming. As I gasped for breath, Ray assured me we were going to be all right.

"I don't think so," I said, breathless.

He said the togetherness would make us all closer and we'd all be okay.

But it wasn't. On that very first night we moved in, it rained, and water was running in the front door on our newly installed carpet.

Chapter Six

O ur business dealt with a very affluent clientele. One day Ray was at a large estate, working on a service in the Philadelphia Main Line, where he met two stonemasons. Their work was outstanding. Ray asked if they would come out to do a walkway for us. This would be the beginning of a four-year relationship. We often joked that it all started with a sidewalk. Anyone that pulled into our driveway in the early days would have thought we did not have a clue as to what we were doing.

I know because there were times when I thought this. They would have seen two masons cutting flagstone and building a walk leading to this little cottage. They would not know that this was to direct the rain water away from the front door so we would not drown while sleeping on the floor!

Craftsman Nick and Vick preparing flagstone to
create a walkway down to the pool.

We had already removed all the windows from the main
house—all forty of them—which I was very reluctant to do. They
were very old, with counterbalances to open and close the windows.
Many of the panes were broken. I gave in to being practical as they
were not heat efficient, and in a home this large, I could not imagine
what our electric bills would be. I did not make this decision lightly.
I have always loved old things. They are reminders of what once was
a much simpler way of life.

I felt privileged to be living here. I was trying to restore this
farmhouse to its former glory but to also stay true to its early past.

Of course, it would be a little while before I told this to my family, who were all still struggling with the trauma of having been uprooted from our once very comfortable life. We were all taking turns having our own breakdowns.

To keep out the rain, we boarded up with plywood the windows that we had just taken out. We ordered new Andersen windows with panes to match the windows in the newer wing of the house, which were in very good condition. The boys only wanted to know where the school bus would stop, terrified of what their friends would think of a boarded-up house. I assured them it wouldn't be out front of the house.

The boys were off from school for the summer. We had been working hard. Most days, either Ray or I would stay home from work. I was bookkeeper for the business.

On this day, we both had to go into work. We were ready to fill up our next dumpster. We had it parked in the paddock of the barn. We had asked young Ray and Mark to start to fill the dumpster from the wing that had fallen down. I had asked them to pack it carefully as we had a lot to put in there. When we arrived home later, I was shocked to find that these kids had put each timber and stacked them so neat as to fill just one small portion of the dumpster. I was so proud of them. I was feeling guilty that they were not out playing. At our last home, which everyone was missing, we would have the pool opened now, and they would have been swimming with their friends.

There was another reason we wanted to keep our boys busy.

It was the seventies, and drugs were everywhere. There were drugs in the schools, and there was even talk about legalizing marijuana. We were worried.

Of course, I had not thought about how hard we would all have to work to accomplish this renovation. When you envision hard work, you don't realize how long it will take. Your brain can't fathom working in the physical sense, and your mind works much faster than your body ever could.

Every time I felt guilty about the boys working so hard, Ray would tell me, "It will make men out of them."

I had to remind Ray that we still had a few years before that would happen—unless they ran away from home first.

We all had jobs, and my job was to strip off all the paint from the windowsills. They were so thick with paint after hundreds of years that there were no more corners left on them. If you put a pencil in the corner of a window, you would lose half the pencil in the paint. We could not get away with a little coat of paint, as the realtor had once suggested.

The messy job of stripping the windows

CHAPTER SEVEN

---✦---

The very first time something happened in the house that unnerved me happened one morning when I was alone. I was on the toilet, of all places, in the small bathroom. It was next to the original master bedroom in the oldest part of the house. All the rugs were gone in the house; they too had made it to the dumpster. The floors were bare and the rooms empty.

I heard someone coming down the stairs from the third floor. The footsteps echoed; they were so heavy. And they were coming fast. I had not closed the bathroom door as I knew I was alone.

I called out as I quickly got off the toilet, "Who's there?"

The footsteps instantly stopped, and I was spooked. I ran out of the bathroom while still pulling up my drawers. I feared being trapped in this little room.

I was standing in the bedroom and again cried out, "Answer me! Who's there?" No one answered!

It was quiet. I slowly walked toward the hallway that went to the third floor. I stood at the bottom of the steps; again I called out. No one answered. I could hear a rustling upstairs, and I tried to gather courage as I went up a few more steps. I felt that I should not go any farther.

It felt like when you're in the movies and the person is slowly walking toward the door and someone is hiding behind it and the whole audience is screaming, "Don't go!" I don't know why, but maybe fear or just plain common sense kept me from going up to the room.

Ray Jr and Mike

Ray Jr, Mike, Mark

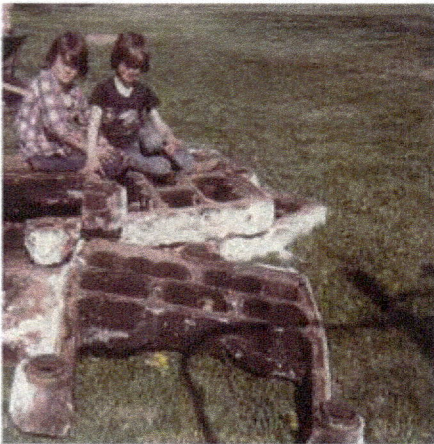

Mark, Mike

We were into major renovations. I was not about to be spooked out of my house. We were spending a fortune, like water pouring out a faucet. We never dreamed it would be so expensive removing trash. I went back to working on the windowsills.

By the end of the day, I had convinced myself that there must be an open window upstairs. A breeze had blown something around. Later that afternoon, I went upstairs. The room was empty, but it could have been branches against the window from the two very large trees outside the house. Of course, they too needed work and would need to be trimmed.

That was as good as I could come up with, and it worked; I felt better. I have always been a practical person, and there would always be a reasonable explanation for everything. However, I would never mention this to my son, Ray, as he wanted this room to be his bedroom. We would have to trim those trees before we moved in.

The next morning, I was again working in the same bedroom, still stripping windows.

This was the bedroom that would have been the master bedroom in the 1700s. Again I was working in the oldest part of the house. This was going to be Mark's bedroom. I was exactly where I had been the day before. No more noise or footsteps, and I was pleased about that. I would spread the stripper on the windowsill, which needed to stay on for twenty minutes. It would buckle the paint and lift it up so you could scrap it off. It was a messy job. While waiting, I decided I would check on the boys.

Ray had them captive in the basement. They were taking out the old knob and tube wiring. Ray told me that when they were finished with that, he would replace all the copper tubing. He was a man possessed, but not the kind like Linda Blair in *The Exorcist*.

It was worse! He started telling me we were going to replace the heater, the one that heated the whole house. Then we would take out the huge water tank and replace it with a new one. This had never been discussed before. I looked past him to the kids. They were making faces as if to say, "Get us out of here, Mom." I was not in the mood for an argument with Ray, so I went back to my window upstairs that was waiting for me.

I walked back up the center staircase to the second floor and passed the stairs that had been the scene of the mystery the day before. I walked past the small bedroom that held the corner hutch and noticed the door was slightly closed.

I pushed open the door and waited to see if it would close again. I wanted to make sure the door was hung properly. It stayed open, and I went back to working on the window. I finished my window and was curious to see if the door stayed open.

It was again partially closed. I stared into the empty room. There was no draft that I could see or feel. There were no open windows. We had not yet taken out the old windows, but there could be drafts that only happened with a slight breeze, I reasoned.

As I stood, deep in thought, the door remained open. I really was not going to dwell on this, so I continued to work on the next window. I was scraping the stripper off to reveal the new wood on the very deep windowsills. I wondered how many years had passed since it had been exposed, like the new wood that was now in front of me.

It still looked brand-new, like it had been preserved from all the layers of paint. I rubbed my hand over the now-cleaned windowsill. I wondered who had planed the wood and how many centuries ago it had been when someone had last run their hand over their work.

I was only a few feet away from the other bedroom door. I could not resist, and I took another look. Again it was slightly closed. Again I pushed the door back to the wall and stood there waiting as if playing a game, but it stayed open. I was not at all spooked that day. The day before, I had felt threatened. It sounded like heavy footsteps coming down the steps.

I finished the last window in what would be Mark's room. I checked the door again in the small bedroom just a few feet away and found it slightly closed.

This time I pushed it open and said loudly, "Knock it off, and leave the door open."

For the remainder of the day, the door remained open. I was quite pleased with myself. Whoever or whatever it was, it listened. I chuckled.

The next morning, I was working on the window in this small bedroom, the same room where I could not keep the bedroom door open the day before. I was scraping off the paint when some stripper hit the wall. I was trying to scrape it off the wall when I noticed something was behind it. I could not believe my eyes. It was a mirror. It was just above the corner hutch. It looked like it had been put there to make a dressing table.

Someone had painted over the mirror the same color as the walls. So this had been a little girl's room at one time. And then they painted it blue for a little boy. One day I would like to research this old house so I could put names to the people who had once lived here.

Mike

Mark

Helping to
strip windows

Young Ray

CHAPTER EIGHT

In the evening, in the cottage, we would sit and eat dinner at our table in our now-cozy living room. We would talk of the events of the day. I was trying to make our life in crisis appear normal. I never once mentioned anything unusual. There was a reason for everything, and although I might never know exactly what that reason was, I was quite sure it was not out of the ordinary. Besides, my boys were too busy complaining about their dad.

"He's lost it, Mom" was becoming a normal phase every night.

It was summer now, and when their dad was at work, they would say things like "Let's put this place back together and sell it so we can get out of here."

I agreed with them—not because of anything paranormal, but because my husband was tearing everything out. The boys were complaining with good reason that we would never be finished if he kept pulling everything apart. Little did I know that our renovation was about to take on a whole new meaning of *disaster*.

Nick and Vick, our new stonemasons, had done a beautiful job on the walk to the cottage. Ray had also asked them to take the walk and continue around the side to the pool area. When I asked why we were doing this now, he answered in an annoyed voice, "Because they are here now, and I want to get it all done."

But in walking to the pool area, you went down a slope. This would now require a retainer wall and steps going down to the pool. Of course, it was being built using only the finest flagstone that money could buy. Ray was not in charge of the checkbook, and this was not something he would ever think to worry about. The retainer wall would run along the back of the cottage and be capped in blue stone. It was truly the most beautiful walk and wall that now overlooked the ugliest pool ever.

View from the inside of the cottage looking toward the pool.

In between doing my windows, we all multitasked. I was getting estimates for new cabinets. I had wanted to take off the side porch and add an addition for an eat-in kitchen. I wanted to knock out the existing wall, which everyone told me was a load-bearing wall, and put in a very large picture window.

I had been told now by five builders that it could not be done. The second floor, they said, would fall down. There would not be enough stone in the corner to support the second floor. The fifth builder had just left when up walked Nick.

He asked in his thick Italian accent, "What's the matter?"

I told him what all the builders had explained, and Nick answered, "What's the big a deal? If it falls down, we'll a pick it back up!"

And that was how we tore down the end of the house.

The end of our farmhouse now looked like a rubble of stone. It looked as if it had been bombed. I don't think a bomb could have done as good a job. Nick and Vick had rescued one of the beams from the barn and had used it to hold up the second floor. The two of them were old-world craftsmen, but they only worked on Saturdays and Sundays, and it would be a long summer putting it back together.

The boys at this point were really complaining. "We had gone too far," they said. They were sure of it. And if that was not enough, their father wanted to put central air in the farmhouse. This meant more work in the basement. Every night I had to assure them we really did know what we were doing. Although at this point, I couldn't be sure.

While the house was at its worst, Ray was now taking up the floors upstairs, only a few floorboards in each room, but you needed to be careful walking or you would go through the floor. He was running new wiring in each room.

I walked out across the floorboards in what one day would be the kitchen to find Ray holding on to a rope. Someone was on the other end, crawling in the crawl space. I asked why he was holding a rope and Ray explained it was tied around little Mike's waist. Just in case he got stuck fishing wires, he could be pulled out. He was using our seven-year-old son to fish wire under the floorboards in the dark, tiny, scary crawl space.

"Oh my god," I cried out, "he's only seven!"

"Well, if he was any older, he'd be too big," said Ray.

"Is this even legal to be using our kids like this?" I gasped.

Of course, little Mike wouldn't complain. He loved playing army. This time, I was sure, he thought of it as a mission he had in enemy territory. It certainly looked like a bombed-out farmhouse in Europe during the war.

I was beginning to believe we would never get this house back together. We now had a carpenter who was boxing in the ducts for the air-conditioning. He was putting them in the corner of the closets so as to air-condition the upstairs. But the closets had no doors on them; they were out, being stripped. And the floors were all up while they fixed the joists in the basement.

Ray had laid big sheets of plywood so you could walk across the floors as you went through the rooms. I could just imagine what the serviceman installing the ductwork must be thinking. There was plywood covering the openings where windows should have been, and there were no kitchen and walls at one end of the house where it looked like a bomb had gone off, but he was there installing air-conditioning ducts.

We needed to start to put back the house. It was now late summer, and the going was slow on the addition.

I asked Ray, "When are we going to start to close up the house?"

"When all the wiring, plumbing, and ductwork are done," he said in an annoyed voice, like I had just asked a stupid question.

Each night I returned home to our cottage and showered. My hair was starting to fall out, and I thought it was my nerves.

"Look I said"—I showed Ray a handful of hair—"I am literally starting to fall apart."

"We don't have time for that!" He answered.

This was the outside view. Before we started it was years of overgrowth

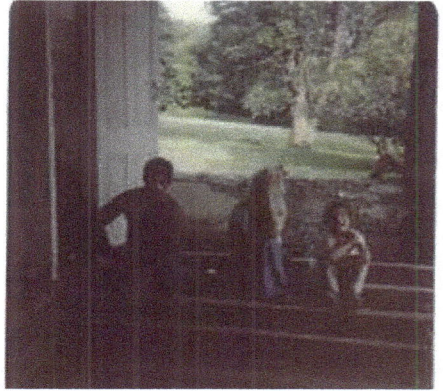

This was the view looking to the outside after we removed everthing

Little Mike reporting for work age 7

Little Mike loading the bucket of the back hoe

Young Ray now holding rope while little Mike carries wires through the crawl space and Ray Sr. giving orders

Chapter Nine

The most popular room in the whole house was the bathroom. It was the only room in the house that you could sit and rest or hide even if only for a while. Ray had some sixth sense that told him one of his troops was slacking. We never knew how he knew; he just did.

It would not be long before he'd call out, "Where are you?" He would accuse us of all having bowel problems and needing to see a doctor.

He always knew where to find me; I would be working on these windowsills until I grew old. Ray decided it would take too long to strip off all the paint from the doors. He decided to take off all the doors in the house, including the front doors, and send them out to be stripped. We also had to remove all the hardware that would need to be cleaned. This was the newer hardware.

The H and L hardware was the old hardware from the original part of the house and was made of forged black steel. We left that on the bathroom doors for privacy. It was this hardware on the small bathroom door that would be involved in the next incident.

It was the same bathroom that I had to make a quick exit from a few days before. One of the kids came to tell us that the small bathroom was locked and no one was inside.

"That's impossible," I said. "The bathroom door has a slide bolt." You would have to lift it up then slide the bolt through a hole and turn it down. The bolt was just like what you might find on a barn door or a stall door. Ray and I went to check the bathroom, only to find it locked. The boys went for the ladder.

Ray had to climb two stories up the outside of the house. As he looked inside the new Andersen window, the bolt had been slid across but not yet put down.

Someone would have had to pick it up in order to slide the bolt across. Ray climbed through the window and slid back the bolt and opened the door. The boys were standing there, all three of them, and from the look on their faces, they wanted an explanation. I thought Ray came up with a good one.

He said, "The humidity in the house had swelled the door. The bolt had just caught the edge of the hole it would pass through. I am sure if you had just jiggled the door a little longer, we could have opened it from the inside."

It sounded good to me, but judging from their faces, I was not sure they believed it.

One day while standing in the window, scraping off the excess stripper, a drop fell on my head. I now knew what was causing my hair to fall out. The stripper had been breaking it off. It had nothing to do with nerves. There was always an explanation for everything. Now I covered my head when I stripped the windows. This was one mystery solved.

CHAPTER TEN

Ray had a friend, George, who was a plumber. He had been working at the house with Nick and Vick at the same time while working on the addition. George was replacing all the copper wiring in the basement and a new water heater. The oil company who we would use for service was also installing a new heater for the home. There were days we had so many people here it sometimes looked like we needed a village to put this house back together.

We were also restoring the wing of the barn. The joists and concrete floor were still intact, so Ray had decided to rebuild the wing and use this part of the barn for our business. We had a back road that came up behind the barn, so it would not interfere with our personal life. Of course, all this building was going on at the same time. This was all being done with one plumber, two stonemasons, one carpenter, and us. The boys were the helpers. Young Ray worked with the carpenter, and Mark worked with Nick and Vick.

Each night, the boys would complain to me who was being worked the hardest. They were learning a lot about the trades, but that didn't mean a thing to them.

One night, we started watching the movie *Roots* when Mike said, "I don't want to watch this. I am living it right now." Mike was the youngest, and everyone asked him to get whatever they needed. He was running all day.

One night while sleeping in the cottage, we would be awakened by the electric mixer turning on in the middle of the night. We had left the mixer on the counter. It had started up all by itself and continued to run until Ray got up and turned it off.

When I asked Ray, how could this happen, he said, "We must have a short." He unplugged the appliance.

All I could think was "Oh, would he want to rip out the wiring in here?" It never ever occurred to me that it could be anything else.

One day the boys found a small plaque. It could fit in the palm of your hand. It looked like it might have come off something, but it was the words that would carry such impact.

We the unwilling, led by the unqualified,
Have been doing the unbelievable
For so long with so little
That we now attempt the impossible
With nothing

The boys knew that it was exactly what was happening to us. I had aligned myself with the boys at this point. It was us—against *him*. We were all in agreement that we were the unwilling, and we would all remind Ray that he was the unqualified. Where this plaque came from will always remain a mystery, but it really summed things up. It would become our motto. We all knew the words by heart. I always wondered why we found it then. Life is all about timing.

Winter was coming fast, and we needed to get the house closed up. We still needed to purchase another forty windows for the barn. The windows had been thrown in the dumpster early on, and all our furniture was being stored in the second floor of the barn, exposed to all the elements. The money was going out the door so fast it was impossible to take account of what we were spending. Ray and I had not had time to argue, and we needed to keep a united front for the kids. We couldn't let them think their parents were falling apart.

One day it was my turn to go to work, and Ray was in the living room with the carpenter. I knew he was going to take up the floors, and we had not had an estimate of what it would cost to replace them. I went in to say good-bye. They were talking about taking up the subflooring so they could plumb the beams below; apparently the joists were out of whack. Some needed to be picked up, and some needed to be lowered.

This was the last straw. The living room floors and the dining room were the only floors left that you could still walk on. I said, "Don't touch the f—— subfloors! They're fine. They've been here for a very long time and don't need touching."

"Okay," Ray answered, not wanting to get into an argument after hearing the hysteria in my voice.

As long as I have been married to Ray, he has never listened to me. I came home later that day, and when I opened up the front door, I was looking down at the basement.

The beams that had been under the floor were still there. They were in the basement, jacking them up, but now I could see the two of them from the front door.

How convenient, I thought, *I only have to look down to talk to them in the basement.*

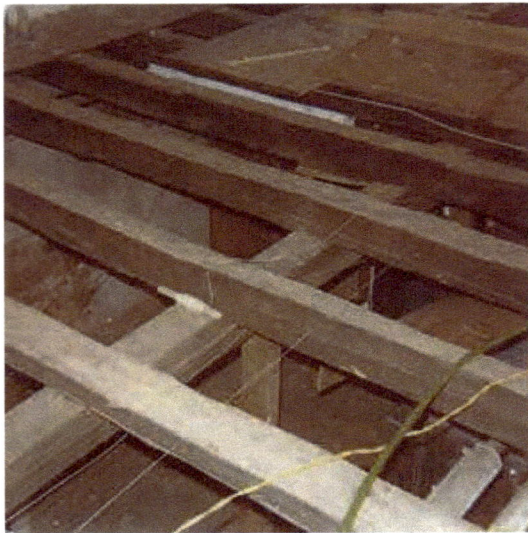

Ray and I just looked at each other. I closed the door without saying a word. That night, you could feel the tension in the room; I couldn't do this to my boys. I wanted to scream at their dad, but I didn't.

Every well has its bottom, and I was looking at my reflection in ours. I let my anger dissolve once again. I did not want to upset the kids. We had enough going on in our lives, and simply put, there wasn't enough time to argue.

What is it about men that whenever you're upset, they think that sex will cure everything? When will they learn it's not a good idea when you're furious? The boys had asked us a few times why their dad called me Sister Mary. Community living had turned me into a nun.

We had tried once in the barn on our mattress that was piled high on bureaus, late at night, but the mattress slid off and us with it. We spent the night trying to lift the mattress back onto the bureaus. We again tried one night in the pasture, where we laid out a blanket, only to be eaten alive with mosquitos. This was how Sister Mary was born.

Chapter Eleven

---⚜---

One Sunday morning while we were all working, we had a visitor. I was still stripping windows when Mark came running upstairs. "The Snellenbergs are here."

They had been the prominent family that we had been hearing about since we had bought the farm. People would say, "When the Snellenbergs had this place, it was a showplace." I would try to explain to them that it would look like that again one day.

However, I would only get a cold stare as they looked around.

When I would give directions for someone on the phone to come out and give us an estimate for any work, they would always say, "Oh yeah, the old Snellenberg place." All this work and all this money, and it was still the old Snellenbergs' place. I wondered if it would always be the Snellenbergs' place. Any wonder my kids thought of them as celebrities.

When I went downstairs, Ray and the boys were busy showing her the house. Ray was explaining what it was that we were doing. It was still in the early stages and needed explaining. My husband introduced me to their daughter who had come to visit. She had grown up in the house and was sharing her memories with my family. She was young and pretty. She looked as if she had just come from lunch at the country club.

I, on the other hand, had stained hands and had wondered if my fingernails would ever look clean again. I had my head covered and had on old stained clothes.

I looked and felt like a slob.

I am not given to jealousies, but at this moment, I was the green-eyed monster. She had heard that the farmhouse was being restored and had wanted to see it again.

I watched as my husband and the boys followed her around like puppies.

I said, "When we are finished, we would like it if you would bring your parents back to visit."

She answered, "My parents got divorced when they lived here, and as far as I know, so has everyone else who ever lived in this house."

Oh, just what I needed to hear. They must have been trying to restore this place too, I thought.

"Well," I exclaimed, "we'll have to break that trend, won't we!" Not knowing what else to say, I said goodbye as politely as I could and went back to work. My family continued following her around while hanging on her every word.

It was the end of summer and time for the boys to go back to school. I called the school, only to find out that the bus would stop right outside the farmhouse. Oh wow, this was not going to be good. Well, we were the talk of the township. Why not the school?

I had actually finished all the upstairs windows. Ray and I decided to stain all the windows instead of painting them. I could not bear to put paint back on them.

I had read that the earliest of settlers had stained windows. The doors were back on and ready for stain. I had stripped all the baseboards and the bookcases upstairs. I had stayed upstairs and done all the work up there first. Ray had all the wiring in, and all the ducts were now under the floorboards.

We had found a small builder with only a helper, and he was now coordinating the openings with Nick and Vick on the largest window that we could put in the opening. I picked out appliances, and for the first time, I felt that we just might finish this place before going bankrupt.

Nick and Vick had built flagstone steps to the kitchen. Of course, they were topped with only the finest blue stone money could buy. I really needed to tell them it would be okay to use something less expensive.

When I mentioned this to Ray, he said, "It's just what I wanted."

"Well," I answered, loudly, "I'd like to drive a Roll Royce, but I realize I can't."

We went to pick out the carpets so they too could be ordered. Everyone was willing to keep it in stock for when we were ready. Of course, everything needed big deposits.

I had always been the money person in the family. Ray would never think to ask, "Can we afford this?" That was my job, he was fond of saying.

We had been living in the cottage for months now. Christmas was almost here. I couldn't imagine spending Christmas in the cottage. We had been working seven days a week. Thanksgiving was the only day we had off. Ray would call it a free day, but he would remind us that it would be one day less before we would move into the big house. We took the boys to a very nice restaurant to celebrate Thanksgiving, where they all fell asleep while waiting for dinner. Try explaining to the waiter why your children are fast asleep.

Christmas came, and I put up a small tree with some presents. Ray gave us another free day, and the boys rode their bikes. Ray and I went back to work. I could see the light at the end of the tunnel, and I was now obsessed. The kitchen was now under a roof, and the stone that had been under all that rubble and stucco was beautiful, Bucks County Fieldstone, and I knew this dated the farmhouse to the early 1700s.

This is what young Ray and his friend had to clean up after a day of chipping stucco.

Young Ray and friend at the end of the day, after cleaning up.

Ray Sr. on Christmas morning.

I had visited some famous homesteads, like the Thompson Neely house at Washington's Crossing and the William Penn Estate on the Delaware River, both in Pennsylvania. The original homesteads were both done in the same stone. The addition had turned out so well with the stone that had been covered for years that I was taking the chisel and hammer and knocking off large areas of stucco all around the outside of the house and everywhere I found stone underneath.

Ray was having a fit. "Don't make any more work for us!" he exclaimed.

Oh, how the tables had turned. It was okay when he was destroying the interior of the home and we wanted to get moved in.

"This is something we can do over the winter," I said.

Ray asked, "But why now?"

I answered in an annoyed voice, "Because Nick and Vick are here now, and I want to get it all done!"

On the second and third floor, we were ready to paint. I had stained all the windows, woodwork, and doors. We picked out a soft cream for all the walls.

I had just remembered the realtor's words. "Just a coat of paint" had taking us eight months. But we were finally here.

We started on the third floor and continued down to the second floor. We had tried to hire a painting crew, but the prices were outrageous. The money was nearly gone.

I had cleaned all the bathrooms. Ray had wanted to rip them all out, but I drew the line here. I made them look like new. We were moving through the top half of the house with lightning speed. The boys were now excited. They had grown so much in these past months and knew we had only days left before we moved in. The carpets went down when we finished painting the top half of the house.

The kitchen was finished with a triple wide window that overlooked the pastures and cottage. It was a beautiful kitchen. The eat-in kitchen area was finished. We finished the ceiling in wood and beams, and it looked great.

We had put a NuTone system for music and intercom with the master unit in the kitchen.

Almost from the first day we installed the system, we had a problem. It had so much static that Ray kept taking the brand-new unit out for service. They could never find anything wrong with it. They replaced the brand-new unit, but still had the same results.

Apparently, the talk-listen button was where all the static was coming from. We had to disconnect the button. The boys joked that someone was trying to talk to us.

At this time, Ray had decided that we would continue to live in the cottage until the rest of the house downstairs was finished. I believe he was waiting for a ribbon ceremony to take place before we could move in. Maybe we could invite the town, and the mayor could do the honors and cut the ribbon, yeah. I knew now what the boys kept saying was true; he really had lost it. He even told us we could not use the kitchen until we were all done with the house. It was to stay brand-new until the day we moved in.

We all looked at him, and then without saying a word, the boys and I went back to the cottage. I said to the kids, "Grab everything you can carry to the big house. It's moving day, boys, and we're moving in."

I had had to put up with a lot since we had purchased this farm—but not today. We were moving in and sleeping for the first night in the big house, and Ray could either step aside or be mowed down.

Before we started

Feb, 1978
Back porch

July 1978

← The new
kitchen
looking
out from
dining
room
doorway

In the
rubble-the
butterfly
steps →
looking
from the
outside

The finished
kitchen and
butterfly
← steps all
carpeted.
On the left
of the step,
the basement
door.

Starting
to look
like a
kitchen

Boys chipping stucco

Lowering bucket of chipped stucco

Young Ray and Nick

Nick mixing concrete

Due to all the construction the circle around the driveway had completely turned to mud. We decided to outlined this area with the cobblestone that Nick had reclaimed from the old streets of Philadelphia.

Ray digging the trench

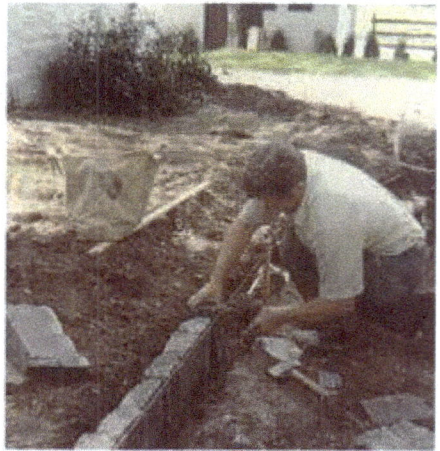

Nick setting up the cobblestone

Starting to take shape

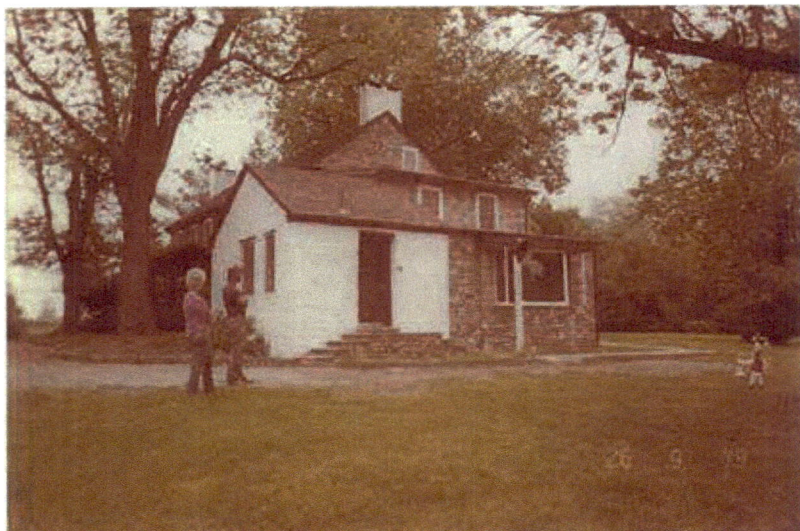

Looking back at all that had been done

CHAPTER TWELVE

It was July 4, 1979. We had been living in the main house now for three months. We had been invited to a Fourth of July cookout. It was by a friend of Mark's. Their parents had asked us to join them. We were still working seven days a week, finishing the first floor, and this would be our first outing since we had bought the place fifteen months ago.

We had all been invited, but Ray, our son, had wanted to stay home. He wanted to ride his dirt bike. I promised I would bring him something back to eat. It was the first time that young Ray would be alone in the house.

We had been at the party a few hours when someone said, "Your son is on the phone."

I answered, but before I could say anything, Ray asked me to come home and get him. I assured him we were coming home shortly.

"No," he said abruptly, "come and get me now." He said this in a frantic voice I had never heard before.

I asked, "What's wrong?"

"I'll tell you when you get here. Just come home now, please."

When I pulled in the driveway, Ray was waiting for me on the steps. He looked shaken.

I asked, "Are you all right?"

"No," he answered. "I fell when I was riding my bike. I hurt my ankle when I fell. I limped back to the house and was soaking my foot in the bathtub in my bedroom. Then I heard you, Mom!" he exclaimed. "You were at the bottom of my bedroom steps, asking me to come down. I could hear the music playing. It sounded like you had brought the party back to the house. I could hear people talking and laughing. I even went to the door and called down to you that I would be down in a minute. I needed a bath because of the fall from my dirt bike. I was muddy. The whole time I was in the tub, and while I dressed, maybe an hour or more, I listened to everyone having a good time. Then I opened the door.

"The second I opened my door to come downstairs, it was dead quiet. At first, I thought that you might be showing them the house. When I got to the second floor, I walked toward your bedroom, but by the time I reached Mark's bedroom, I knew it was too quiet. Mom, all the music was gone, and the voices had disappeared. Where did everyone go? It was beginning to feel creepy. By now," he continued, "I was expecting someone to jump out and scare me at any minute.

"It felt like someone was watching me and playing a game. I went down the center-hall staircase with my back against the wall. By the time I reached the first floor, I could hardly get my breath. I was so scared now. I knew, Mom, I was alone, but I still felt like something was there with me. Where could everyone have gone? I had been listening to everyone partying for almost an hour, and now there was nothing but silence. I was so scared. If I could have pulled the phone off the wall and taken the phone outside to call you, I would have. *Mom, what's in our house?*"

I believed him. We had all been having a few things happen to each of us, but nothing of this magnitude. It was shortly after this when my mother-in law Marge would pass away. Debbie was my husband's youngest sister. She alone had cared for Mom. In Ray's family, there were four sisters and one brother. We had all tried to help Debbie. She lived at home with Mom and would look after her like a nurse. Marge, my mother-in-law, was dying of a brain tumor, and Debbie was afraid that the rest of us would put Mom in a home.

That was exactly what happened in the end. She was only there for a few days when she passed away. We all assured Debbie she had done the very best for Mom that anyone could have done. Debbie was emotionally exhausted. We agreed that she should come and live with one of us. We all wanted to help her get back on her feet. Debbie asked to live with us.

It would not be long before Debbie would learn that we were not alone in our home. I knew that Debbie was crying every night. I understood her loss. I think everyone remembers the day they lost their mom. I wanted to cry with her, but I didn't feel I should intrude on her time of grief. It was such a private moment.

When I look back at this time, I can't believe it took me so long before I would acknowledge that there was indeed someone else living here. Even young Ray's experience was something I had placed on the back burner of my mind. We had been working for so long that I wouldn't let anything or anyone keep us from finishing this house or chase us out. That was not going to happen.

Debbie would come down in the morning and tell me stories of the night before. She would tell me she could feel his presence in her room. When she was in bed, she said, he would play with her covers down by her feet. When she would shower in the morning, she would come back and find the bed she had just made was messed, as if someone had laid down on it.

I am sorry to say that I would tease her.

My teasing was meant only jokingly. I was very fond of Debbie and wished I could do more to help her through her pain. Debbie learned to tell me about him like it was a joke. One morning, she told me that she had given him a name.

"What did you name him?" I asked with a big smile on my face.

"I call him Seymour." said Debbie.

"Why do you call him Seymour?" I wanted to know.

"Well, think about it!" she said. "He sees more of everything."

We both laughed.

CHAPTER THIRTEEN

D ebbie lived with us for about a year and had many stories. It was shortly after she moved out that I would call her to say I was sorry. I wish I had listened more to what she was saying. It would be a pivotal moment for me when I would come face-to-face with what most of us now referred to as Seymour.

Aunt Debbie taking little Mike to school.

The same events that had happened to Debbie would happen to me one evening.

Ray and I had been working hard for a very long time. We had experienced some of the most difficult times of our lives. We had run out of money long before we had finished the house. Ray, an avid car lover, had to sell his '32 Ford Roadster. It was sold to help finish the house. We had been arguing for some time.

Although the kids could not hear us now that we were in the house, there was no mistaking the tension. It took a strong mindset to keep working like we had been working. We had not taken the time to see how far we had come; there was only how much we still had to do. There were a great many people who didn't make it through this kind of renovation, and it looked like we might be one of them. On this evening, everything came to a head. I had *had it*!

I was tired of being told what to do each day and how to do it. I had been putting up with this for a very long time now, and I was browbeaten. The main house was all finished, and I knew we could sell for a profit and go our separate ways. This idea looked better to me all the time, and now I wanted out! I had packed my clothes. It had been coming for a long time. Ray now decided he wanted to talk things out.

He had started a fire in the fireplace of the newly finished library. This was a first for him—wanting to talk things out. The boys were out for the evening. He had not spoken to me for more than a year. He had only shouted orders. I must admit that when we were up against it, Ray had been the force to keep us all going. He had let up on the strong-arm tactics on the boys by now, but I was still his slave. Now he wanted us to talk it out this evening.

It would turn out to be a very strange evening. It started out okay. We poured a glass of wine and sat by the fire in the library for the first time. The poignant moment only lasted a short time. Before long, all the anger had come back. We were screaming at each other. I had always been one to talk with my hands, and as I waved my hands in the air, I was getting shocks on the tips of my fingers. It hurt. It felt like the static you got when touching a light switch just after walking across a carpet, but I was still sitting. Ray waved his hand, and I could see the static as blue light. I left the room angry. I went upstairs and lay down on our bed. I started to cry, and this was when I felt it.

Someone had just crawled over me. I felt a presence just an inch above my face. I bolted straight up off the bed, and fear gripped me as I looked around the room. I thought, *Ray could not have moved that quickly. What kind of game is he playing?*

It was impossible for anything to have moved that quickly. I moved slowly toward the door, expecting Ray to jump out at me. I went down the back staircase with my back against the wall. I didn't know what I was expecting, but I was terrified. I could now see Ray sitting by the fire in the library, unaware that I was standing there, staring at him. I walked in and sat down. I explained to him what had just happened to me. He listened with a look of complete disbelief.

I had supposed that he thought I made this all up to have an excuse to come down and talk to him. Oh, he was so arrogant. We talked for a moment about this, but it would not be long before we were fighting.

The static in the room was now getting stronger. As we waved our arms about, we were both getting shocked, strong shocks; however, it would take a bolt of lightning to stop this argument. I stormed out of the room and back upstairs. I was fueled to end this now. I started packing, and just then I heard a loud gunshot. It was as loud as a double-barreled shotgun.

I must admit I had thought Ray might have shot himself. I am not sure if, at that moment, I was upset. It sounded like it was just under me in the library. I started running down the stairs; Ray was running out of the library, screaming, accusing me of smashing something upstairs. We met on the staircase, and for the next minute, we were both screaming at each other. Then suddenly, we both realized that neither of us had done anything.

I will say that this was the beginning of us talking. We walked back into the library and sat down. At first, we talked about what had just happened and then about everything, and not once was there any static in the room. The static was gone. We were really tired now. We went to bed with no more events that evening.

The next morning, things between us seemed to get better. We both agreed that if we ever wanted to fight again, we would rent a room somewhere, anywhere, just not here. Ray had never believed in anything paranormal. All he would agree to was that it had been a strange evening.

After that night, Ray and I continued to improve our relationship. I had always believed that in order for Ray to acknowledge that there might be something going on in the house, he would first have to think about what might be after death. And this was a subject he was not going to deal with or discuss—ever.

I thought back to what Debbie had told me about her experience with Seymour. He was known to all of us by his name now. Debbie had said she had felt someone come over her, and I wondered if she had been crying at that time.

Was this the catalyst that brought him to comfort you?

It had been so unbelievable that I had trouble acknowledging this when Debbie had told me until now when it happened to me. When I spoke to Debbie by phone for the first time about this, I could hear it in her voice; she felt vindicated. I now knew what she had known. I vowed never to cry again in this house, and I never did.

Could it be sorrow that brought it out to console you?

CHAPTER FOURTEEN

---❦---

I had a few days now to think about what might have taken place the other night. I had come to the conclusion, in a practical way, that there might be a scientific explanation for what had happened.

Albert Einstein was quoted as saying, "Time is just a place." This statement had always fascinated me. A place can be visited many times.

Could the shot we had heard the other night be a shot that had been fired years ago? The wing of the house we had been standing in had been built in the fifties. In the 1800s, we would have been standing outside the house, and someone might have just shot a deer or bird for dinner.

The door that kept closing in the hallway could have been someone else closing that same door in another era. Maybe that person in this other era was also wondering why that same door would not stay closed.

And the heavy footsteps coming fast down the steps in the early days of renovations could have been some farmer's son coming down for breakfast in his heavy work boots. This idea was less alarming and more comforting. I was not ready to deal with the presence that had climbed over me and was just above my face as I lay in my bed.

I had all but convinced myself that we were experiencing many things from another era. This idea didn't last long when the following event happened. This would happen to me when I was once again alone. We had all been working this Saturday, mowing all the pastures, which took all of us most of the day. We had mowers for everyone.

It made the farm look like a sprawling estate, but there was always a mower going. When all the work was done, not one of the boys stayed around. They were off with their girlfriends or out riding their bikes with friends.

On this late afternoon, we had ordered takeout food, and Ray had gone to pick it up. I was in the bathroom at the other end of the house when I heard loud music coming from another room. I was slowly walking through the house, and it was getting louder. It was so loud it was hurting my ears. I stepped down into what was now our TV room. *Saturday Night Dance Fever* was blaring on the new TV. The volume had been turned up all the way. We had made the small room over the kitchen our TV room and had purchased a Sony TV.

It was hidden in a box, and when you turned on the remote control, it would rise up out of this box and turn on. I turned the volume down and called out to see if anyone was in the house. No answer. I turned off the TV and watched it close up again. I put down the remote and was walking toward the small step to go back to my bedroom when the TV went on again. The volume was again turned up all the way. I quickly turned off the TV and turned the volume all the way down. I stared at the box for a long time, still trying to make out what was going on. I held the remote in my hand and then set it on the coffee table. I slowly turned and walked to leave the room. It again went on as loud as ever. I quickly turned down the volume. This time, I sat down for a minute to see what would happen next. Married to an electrical contractor, I was thinking there was a short in the TV or receptacle.

Nothing happened. I waited while I watched *Dance Fever*. I again turned off the TV and waited for what seemed like five minutes. But as I got up and started to leave the room, I turned back to see the TV going on with the volume turned all the way up. I was now spooked.

I had not felt this way from the time I had run out of the bathroom or when I felt the presence that came to me one night, which I had yet to deal with, and here I was once again feeling fear. There was no doubt in my mind—I was being watched. It was playing games with me. There was no mistake; there was something or someone there with me, watching me, at that moment.

My reaction to fear was anger. I have been this way my whole life, and this was no exception. With fear, you have two choices—flight or fight. I would always choose to fight. I found myself screaming at whoever or whatever was there. I was enraged and ready to do battle.

I turned off the TV remote and screamed, "Leave it alone! Don't mess with me, or you'll be thrown out on your ass one way or another!"

This said, I went quickly down the butterfly steps to the kitchen and waited outside on the kitchen steps for Ray to come back with the food. It reminded me of the time when young Ray waited outside on the steps for me to come and get him. The TV never went on by itself again unless someone in the house turned it on. Of course, I told Ray all that had just happened. He listened and as usual had no comment.

I was still talking about this event and others when we were in bed that evening. Ray asked, "What one room, in the house, would we find Seymour?"

I thought for a moment, and I suspected the small bedroom with the little girl's vanity might be where he stayed. Most of the activity was in the center area of the home in the oldest part of the house. Ray suggested we go to his room and ask Seymour what he was up to.

I knew Ray was teasing me, but I wondered what might happen if we did this. The boys were fast asleep. It was about 1 a.m. in the morning when we walked into the room where the corner dressing table was; in the room that had been made for a little girl.

Ray asked, in his rugged voice, "Are you here, Seymour?"

To this day, we still cannot explain what it was that we both heard in the middle of that night. It was the sound of children giggling.

Ray and I stood there without saying a word and stared at each other in stunned silence. We both moved toward the door and left the room still silent as we went down the hallway to where Mark and

Mike were sleeping. We stood there wondering what we had just heard when Mark woke up startled. We assured him everything was okay and told him to go back to sleep.

Mark and Mike were sleeping in the same bedroom in twin beds. They had all wanted their own bedroom before we moved in. It was a six-bedroom home, but now Mike did not want his own room. I didn't blame him. Ray would have to believe that Seymour was real now as we both heard the same thing, but it was the sound of children that now had me startled. Just how many souls were living here?

CHAPTER FIFTEEN

W e were still working on the house, but it was at a normal pace now. We had gone from being the neighborhood gypsies who had moved into a pool house to the new owner of this estate. I had validation of this one day when Ray was mowing and I was cleaning. A gentleman showed up in the driveway. He said he was there for an estimate and asked me what the owners who lived here were like to work for.

I smiled and said, "They're very nice to work for, so you can give me the estimate." He would never know the compliment he had just paid me.

I missed having a dog. I have always loved animals. And it had been almost two years since our dog Jet was put to sleep. I was ready to love another dog once again. I never said anything to Ray. He would have had a million excuses as to why we were not ready, so one morning, I drove to the SPCA. Here was where I first saw him—a young Doberman, black and tan, with his ears straight up and his tail docked. He was beautiful. He was staring back at me with the saddest eyes. I called him over to pet him, and he approached me with caution. As I stroked his head through the chain link, I wondered what asshole had put him in here. Of course, I went home with him that day. Ray never said a word; he only asked if I had named him yet. We decided to call him Max.

Dobermans were so regal looking, and he needed a strong name. The boys really liked him, and after only a few days, it was like we had Jet back with us. He slept with the boys, and we all agreed he reminded us of Jet. He was so well behaved. I wondered what his life might have been before us. Why would someone give up this fine-looking dog whose temperament was just as beautiful? One day while running for pure joy in the pasture, he suddenly stopped. I could tell he was in a panic as he looked around. Then I realized he had lost sight of me.

When I called his name, he ran as hard as he could back to me, and I knew then I loved him dearly. All the love I had felt for Jet was back. I took him to the vet to have him checked out. We gave him all his shots just in case he had never had them as a puppy. But it was to be short-lived.

Max had been living with us for about six weeks now. One morning as I came into the kitchen, he was lying on the floor in a full-blown seizure. His eyes were oscillating, and he had lost all control of his bowels, and in the middle of all this, he was trying to give me his paw. I grabbed hold of it and assured him of how much he was loved. After he came out of it, I wiped him off and held him close and cleaned up after him. I was on the way to the vet in a matter of minutes following his attack. He would never come home again.

He had canine distemper. Whoever had him before never gave him his shots when he was a puppy. He had caught this disease when he had gone into the kennel. Of course, the vet notified the SPCA that they had a problem. The shots we had given him were no good. I didn't give up quickly. The virus hit the brain and then attacked the body. Could he survive this without being paralyzed? I asked the vet to wait and see if he would be one of the lucky ones. I should have kept him home with me; it was where he felt safe.

The vet called me; he had several seizures after I left and was paralyzed. I went back and held him in my arms for a very long time and cried. I told him how lucky we were to have had him with us. I let the vet put him to sleep while he slept in my arms.

I never want to forget him. He was someone special. I was reminded of a poem by Rudyard Kipling, "The Power of a Dog."

I will recap the last paragraph.

Our loves are not given, but only lent,
At compound interest of cent per cent,
Though it is not always the case, I believe,
That the longer we've kept 'em, the more we do grieve:
For, when debts are payable, right or wrong,
A short-time loan is as bad as a long-
So why in heaven (before we are there)
Should we give our hearts to a dog to tear? (Rudyard Kipling)

He left his mark on my heart, and I will remember him forever!

CHAPTER SIXTEEN

W e were now working on putting up floodlights on the front of the house. The house had never had floodlights before. Ray and the boys were working all day. I was excited. I wanted to see what the stone on the house would look like lit up at night. The first night we turned them on, we left them on for security. Everyone was pleased, especially the boys, as the light softly illuminated the bedrooms at night. We had just gone to bed for the night when the new lights went off.

The switch was in the hallway just outside the library downstairs. I went downstairs to turn them back on. The switch had been in the off position. I went back upstairs to get back into bed when they went out again. I looked at Ray and, without saying a word, went back downstairs and turned them on again. It had been a while since we had had any problems in the house. Seymour had not been around for a while. Not since, I had screamed at him about the TV.

This was the third time I was turning on the lights, and I waited and stared at the light switch to see if anything would happen. And just like before, nothing happened. I knew it would not happen again until I was back upstairs.

I was just at the top of the steps when my son called out from his bedroom, "It's him, isn't it?"

"No," I answered. "It might be a bad switch."

I asked Ray if that was possible. He answered, "Anything is possible. Is the switch in the off position?"

"Yes," I answered.

The lights were out again.

Ray said jokingly, "If that switch is in the off position, I am getting out of here." He laughed. He could afford to laugh. He wasn't the one going up and down the steps. I again was in the hall just outside the library. The light switch was in the off position.

I turned the switch on, and this time in a very threatening voice said between clenched teeth, like I was snarling, "Leave the lights on *now*! Do not touch them again." The lights remained on for the rest of the evening, and we did not have any more trouble with them ever.

I wondered, "Did they have light switches in the 1800s?"

We had gone a few months without any incident. Now he was back playing with the lights. We also knew he wouldn't stop there. These pranks of his seemed to come in waves. We were sure we'd have a few more things happen before he would take a break. There was a pattern to these episodes. We did not have to wait long. A few nights later, Ray Sr. and I, along with our son Mark, came home after dark. We walked into the kitchen, and the basement door was vibrating back and forth. It had a little play in the handle when it was closed.

It was at this moment shaking with such force that the door was humming. I had never seen anything like it. We all stopped to stare.

Then Ray said with a laugh, "I'm getting out of here." Ray quickly climbed the stairs.

Mark screamed with laughter, "Wait for me!"

Just then, I grabbed Mark off the first step and said, "Not before me."

Mark and I kept pulling each other off the stairs and were laughing while pulling each other down. It was one of those moments you'd remember forever. We didn't know when the door stopped shaking; we had been too busy laughing.

Later that evening, I couldn't help thinking, *Poor Seymour. I was either screaming at him to leave, or we were making fun of him. What's a poor ghost to do?*

I now had come to believe that he was real, but I was not going to let any one of us talk about him outside the house. I was not willing to give our home a reputation—that it was haunted.

Of course, that didn't last either. Young Ray had made friends with some neighborhood boys that had dirt bikes like his. They would ride for hours. One day when they had all come back to the house, they would tell me that they had smelled cigar smoke in the dining room. I had also smelled the scent. But it wasn't cigar smoke; it was a pipe. And it was a sweet smell. It smelled like vanilla.

One of the men who worked for our company had a pipe. It was the same smell I had smelled in the house. He told me they had been making that same tobacco since the early 1800s. I never mentioned why I asked. But soon after that, I bought two large vanilla candles and put them on the end of the buffet, one at each side.

When someone said they smelled cigar smoke or a pipe, I'd simply say, "Oh, it's the vanilla candles I have sitting on the buffet."

Little did I know I had set the stage for another event and would be grateful that the house hadn't burned down!

Pictured is the finished pointed stone farmhouse with
new lighting and shutters at the holidays.

The house outside and inside was now finished.
This is the front on that Thanksgiving day.

The back of the house finished on Thanksgiving day
and our first holiday to celebrate with family.

CHAPTER SEVENTEEN

It was our third Thanksgiving in our house. I never remembered the second because we were still working round the clock. The house was now finished inside.

The downstairs woodwork had all been stained. The pictures were hung and drapes softened the windows. New hardwood floors were down and new carpets were in the library. We had chipped the plaster off the house to reveal the stone and had worked all winter. The boys had a pulley system when filling the buckets with the old plaster and lowering it to the other one waiting with the wheelbarrow.

The house was now a pointed stone farmhouse. My aunt Heather had come to visit when we were early in the construction, and I could see the fear in her face that we had taken on an insurmountable task and would be years before we finished—if we could ever finish. This would be her first time back and our first holiday in our home with family for dinner.

Everyone was shocked. We had finished it. There were still many things to do on the barn and landscaping, but we now had a home—and most importantly had not gone bankrupt.

In celebration of this, we hired a local artist to paint an oil painting of the house. She started it in October, and it was finished by Thanksgiving. We hung it above the buffet in the dining room. As we studied the picture, we realized she had left off a very large tree in the front of the house.

In the Colonial days, it was customary to plant two trees in the front of the house on either side of the doors. This represented the grandparents. In those days, they were the monarchs of a family and held in great esteem. I was disappointed that one of the silver maple trees had been left out of the picture. The artist explained that it hid too much of the house, so she left one of them off.

The turkey had been cooking in the oven all day. My cousin was there with his girlfriend, and as we sat around the table, we gave thanks for all we had come through and were now sharing with family for the first time in years. We had taken a lot of pictures during the day. We even took pictures of the new oil painting hanging over the buffet. When the evening came to an end, we said good-night to our family.

I walked back into the dining room over to the large candles still burning on the buffet. They had been burning all through dinner and into the evening. I blew out the first candle. It had only burned a few inches. I went to blow out the other candle on the other end of the buffet, and it had melted all the way to the bottom. It was a pile of melted wax still burning on the end of the buffet.

It would not have been much longer before it would have set the buffet table on fire. A large twelve-inch candle was gone. I stood there, amazed, wondering how it could be that two large candles that had been lit at the same time would have only one melted a few inches while the other almost completely disappeared. It was only a six-foot-long buffet.

Ray had walked in, and as we stood there, he decided there must have been a draft in the corner of the room, although there was no window or door in this corner and this was the darkest part of the dining room. We developed and picked up the pictures from our holiday meal. We noticed that in one of the pictures we had taken of the oil painting hanging over the center of the buffet, right next to the buffet where the candle had burned the fastest, there was a stream of light.

Could we have captured Seymour on film? Did he spend the holiday with us? Something had caused a draft in that corner of the dining room for the candle to burn down that fast.

During the summer following that Thanksgiving, you can imagine my surprise when a summer storm and a bolt of lightning took out one of the silver maple trees in the front of the house, the exact one missing in the oil painting. The painting now matched the front of the home. I have no explanation except to say that the artist might have been able to predict the future, or did someone whisper in her ear that it would not be there very long?

Could this be Seymour captured on film? The candle on the right burned down until only melted wax was left burning on the buffet.

Chapter Eighteen

It had been three months since Max had died. I had called the SPCA and asked them to call me when they had another Doberman come in. I also added he could be someone that would not be a good candidate for adoption. They, Dobermans, had such a bad reputation. It was harder for these dogs to get good homes.

I did not have to wait long. I got a call and was told they had a three-year-old male who had been part of a legal case of abuse. The case was settled, and he was now available for adoption, if I wanted to come and see him. I went to have a look. What a pitiful sight greeted me. He was so underweight his body was a skeleton of what a dog once looked like. His eyes never met mine. He only looked away in the distance.

It appeared to me he wasn't even there. Only his body remained still breathing. I took his leash when it was handed to me. As I walked him around outside, I was really struck by his absence. He didn't connect with me at all. He only stared off into space. He had several bald spot on his legs, and he was really a poor sight, but I knew I was his only chance. I adopted Max number two that day.

I had never liked it when someone would lose their beloved pet and give the same exact name to the next dog or cat, but there I was doing the same thing. My reasoning was that the first Max had such a short time on this earth that perhaps I could give him another chance at life through this dog. At least, that was what I had hoped. I had a big dog cushion on the floor for him to lie on in the kitchen. It was the room with all the activity and family. I noticed that Max had come back from his faraway look.

He now seemed to look around the room for the first time. He had been lying on that cushion for about four hours. He was checking out his surroundings. Just then, Mike walked past him. I noticed Max curling back his lip. But he had looked away from Mike when he walked past him.

Oh, what had I brought home to my family?

Mark had also noticed this. He asked, "Oh, what can we do with this one?"

We were always rescuing something, so this was one more challenge we had facing us. We agreed we couldn't raise our voices in anger. We were sure he had that his whole life. I am not sure any trainer would agree with what we did next, and no one remembers who it was that made the suggestion that we tell him "how pretty his teeth were."

Every time Max showed us his teeth, we told him in a very soft voice how pretty he was. Of course, we told everyone in the family to use caution when feeding, not to stare him down, and all the things that most of us knew were common sense. How confusing this must have been for this poor soul.

The following just illustrates to me how intelligent dogs are. I can't say for sure just how long it took before we noticed his stubble of a tail started to wag. His snarl had now turned into a smile. When he wanted attention, he would raise his lip and walk around the kitchen, waiting to hear how pretty he was. In short, he went from a shriveled-up prune to a bud unfolding like a flower; he blossomed.

Max was becoming part of our household. We still used caution. I was sure it would take some time, perhaps years, before we erased all his demons. Max liked to sleep on the bottom step in the kitchen. We needed to let him know when we were about to step over him to go back up the stairs. If you tried to step over him while he was still asleep, he would be startled and would grab your leg with his teeth. He never hurt anyone, but you can imagine why you'd want to let him know that you were about to step over him and make sure he was awake. We could all see a side of him that I was sure no one had ever seen, not anyone, from his tortured past.

He was joyful. He now felt safe, loved, and his happiness was felt by all of us. We would now laugh out loud when he raised his lips. He smiled as wide as he could. I am sure he loved the sound of that laughter. There is no greater feeling of satisfaction when you have saved not just a dog but any living thing. The gratitude that they feel can be heartfelt by both. He was with us for a few months when he was joined by a friend.

We had put up 550 feet of fencing that ran along the road. We had a gate at the end of the driveway. This was where the boys were picked up by the bus for school. While waiting for the school bus was when they first saw her. The boys kept telling us there was a small tan dog outside the fence.

On the second day, Ray and I walked out to check and see if the dog was still there.

She was, and when we approached her, she took off across the street. She ran down a dirt road. It led to nursery stock that belonged to an orchard. The dirt road was used only for trucks to go in and dig up trees or shrubs for the landscape nursery to sell. The nursery was about five miles away, and there were no buildings down this dirt road. Ray knew this as well as I, but he tried to convince me that she was heading home.

The next day, my son didn't see her. I was sorry we did not try harder to catch her, but I thought she might have moved on, looking for her home. It was now Saturday, and we were taking a day trip to go up the mountains, just like a real family. It was a cold, damp day in March with showers. When we pulled out of our driveway and turned left, we didn't see her. Then as we drove past where she had been last seen, she came out from under a large Douglas fir tree. This large tree had been giving her shelter. She had been hiding under there, waiting, but for what?

I now believed she had been dumped on the side of the road and she was waiting for them to return. Ray, of course, would not turn around. He had his day planned for a family trip and wasn't changing course. We drove up to a lodge in the mountains and had lunch. All we talked about was the dog. We agreed, the boys and I, that she was ours. It was now about four days since she had first been seen, and she had to be hungry. This would be the way we would catch her.

When we arrived home that evening, I sent Mark out with a can of dog food. It had started to rain; he would be out there for what seemed an hour. She did not give up her freedom easily. Just about the time I was going to send out a search party for my son, he opened up the backdoor. Mark walked through the door and, looking back, coaxed her to come inside, still holding the can of dog food and gently telling her it was okay.

She had taken some dog food from his hand, and it had taken all this time to encourage her to follow him. She was so timid. Once inside, I warmed a towel to dry her off while Mark teased me about not getting one for him. He too was soaked to the bone. We quickly made her feel at home, and I saw instantly that she was a hit with Max. She looked like she might have had some Corgi in her. She had short legs and sandy-blond coat and long flappy ears. Her eyes were sad and sullen.

I had baskets hanging from the ceiling for decoration, and she kept looking up, as if something might fall on top of her. She ate a good dinner that night, and it was probably the first one in several days. The fact that she stayed alongside of the road in that one spot for days convinced me that she had been waiting for someone to return for her.

As I dried her off, it became clear why she did not leave. She was a nursing mom and still had milk for her puppies.

Someone had dumped her on the side of the road, and only God knew what became of her puppies. She was missing them so much that she waited for that one person to come back and return her to her babies. It never ceased to amaze me the cruelty of some humans. Why could they not have taken her to a shelter with her brood so she could have stayed with them and cared for them until they were adopted?

Puppies were always in demand. The fact that she had so much milk led me to believe that they were still very young, so I did not give much hope that they were even alive.

It might just be that she was the lucky one. It would be a long time before she felt like that. I wanted to call her Sandy because of her color, but she deserved a more regal name, so she became Sandra. I took her to a vet, and she had all her shots and spayed at the same time. It took some time for her to recover. I am sure it was a shock to her system, and her grieving heart didn't make it any easier.

Max did what he could to comfort her, and slowly over time, she began to heal and feel loved. And she was loved by all of us. She would turn out to be the most polite and well-behaved little lady I had ever known.

We went out of our way to make this little girl feel special.

I wondered if the two of them, Max and Sandra, would be able to see Seymour the next time he showed up. I wondered how they would have acted in the kitchen with the basement door banging back and forth on that evening.

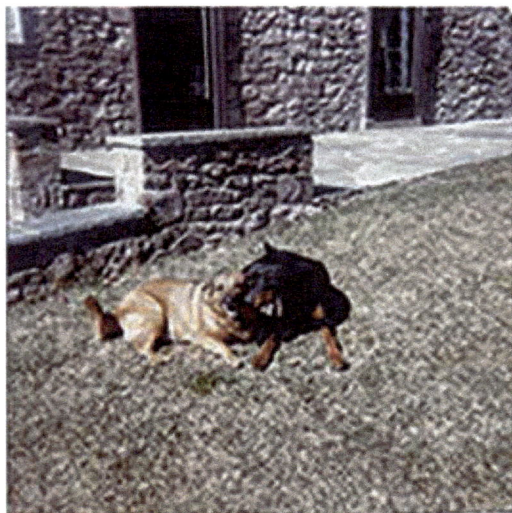

Max and Sandra

CHAPTER NINETEEN

One day while I was cooking in the kitchen, Mark came down the stairs and into the kitchen.

In a whispered voice, he said, "Mom, you need to see this."

He led me back upstairs to the small bedroom, the one with the vanity and the mirror. It was the mirror that had been painted over, the one I had uncovered while stripping the windows.

It was sweating with moisture, as if someone had just gotten out of a shower. I stared at it, not being sure what could cause this. I walked down the hall to the bathroom. It was the same bathroom that I had had to run out of when the footsteps were heard coming fast down the stairs. It was the same bathroom that had locked us out a few years ago.

No one had taken a shower.

There was no moisture on the bathroom mirror. The shower curtain was dry. We again walked back to the mirror in the bedroom. It was a sunny day in spring. There was no humidity. I tried to wipe off the moisture with a paper towel but to no avail.

This room was right next to young Ray's stairs, which led to his bedroom on the third floor. It was the steps that still held the mystery of the heavy footsteps. It was the same bedroom that Ray Sr. and I had gone into in the middle of the night to confront Seymour and where we heard children giggling. This was definitely Seymour's territory. Although he made his presence known in other parts of the house, this had to be where he hung out.

Mark asked, "What do you think it means?"

"I think he's letting us know he's back," I answered.

This would be all Debbie would need to hear. She had told me some time ago when I discovered the mirror that had been painted over to match the walls that when I stripped away the paint, I had somehow released his spirit. It was a great idea for a ghost story, but did I believe it? No. This story, however, would be proof positive for Debbie.

I knew we would not have to wait long before he made his presence known.

I had never told any of my sons about my experience in my bedroom. I still had trouble dealing with this myself, yet it had happened to Debbie. We had kept this to ourselves; I did not want my sons worried about going to sleep in their bed and someone joining them. This was the one place you should feel safe and secure. That was why the following story, which was told to me by young Ray, would be taken seriously by me.

This is the account of what happened to young Ray and would involve Mark and Mike before it was over.

"Mom, I woke up in the middle of the night being held by someone. I could feel his arm lying across me as he held me. I tried to shake him off, but he was wrapped around me. I knew I was screaming but couldn't hear myself. I felt his body around me, holding me. The more I struggled, the tighter he held me. I fell out of my bed backwards on the floor, kicking the covers off, still struggling to get him off. He was still holding my arm when I ran down the stairs and along the hall to Mark's room, screaming, 'Get him off of me! Get him off of me!" Mark, who had been sound asleep, jumped up on his bed and was brushing me off saying, 'Ray, there is no one holding you. There is no one here.'"

And he continued to brush off what he could not see. Mark showed Ray that the arm he had been holding across his body was his own arm. Mark assured his older brother that he must have fallen asleep on his arm. That was why he could not feel it. Mark helped to calm his brother down and assured him he must have been dreaming.

They sat on Mark's bed and continued to talk until Mark and Mike, who were now both wide awake, assured Ray that he must have been having a nightmare. Ray, on the other hand, tried to convince both of them that something had been holding him in bed, that he was wide awake when he ran into their room. But before long, they had managed to convince their brother, Ray, that he had dreamed all of it. Still shaken, young Ray spent the night sleeping on the floor between Mark's and Mike's beds.

They did not mention any of this to me. It was only in casual conversation with my son Ray that I learned of his nightmare. I did not say anything to him other than it must have been a nightmare.

Ray would never know of the experience that both his aunt Debbie and I had felt. If Ray had known that it could have been Seymour with him that night, there would have been three boys sleeping in the same room.

CHAPTER TWENTY

Seymour had made his presence known with the moisture on the mirror. Whenever there was an incident, it would be followed with something else. And young Ray knew nothing of the moisture on the mirror. We never got to talk about the events that happened to us as we were busy going to work and school. After school, the boys had either mowing or now worked in the business. Ray Sr. had no time for stories. We learned to keep these events to ourselves.

It would only be a few nights later when I would be awakened to a sound I did not recognize. I lay there at first, trying to figure out what the sound was and where it was coming from. It was coming from Mark and Mike's bedroom. I walked the short hallway with the buzzing getting louder.

I opened their bedroom door and asked, "What's going on?"

They were still in their beds with the covers pulled up around their necks.

Mark answered, "It's Mike's army tank, and it's driving itself across the desk."

"Why didn't you pick it up and stop it?" I asked.

"It's not my tank," answered Mark in a high-pitched voice.

"And what about you, Mike?" I asked.

"I'm not moving from this bed," answered Mike.

I walked over and picked up the tank, and it stopped. It had been stalled by some books lying on the desk but was still trying to move.

I asked Mike, "How does this tank operate?"

Mike said, still hiding under the covers, "It works by remote control."

"And where is the remote control?"

"It's behind you, Mom, on the bureau."

I looked at the remote and tried to operate the tank.

Mike said, "It needs batteries. I haven't been able to use it. I was going to tell you I needed batteries for my remote."

It was about three o'clock in the morning. I was tired, but a smile crossed my face as I looked at my two sons lying in bed with the covers pulled so tightly around their necks; it must have been hard to breathe. They were both karate kids.

They practiced their katas all the time, and here were my fierce warriors curled up in their beds like it was the safest place in the world to be. No one had wanted to venture out of bed to stop the tank driving itself across the desk.

Mike asked me to leave the bedroom door open, and as I turned to leave their room, I said good night to the boys and added, "Say good night, Seymour. It's time to go to sleep."

CHAPTER TWENTY-ONE

W e lived in a very historic area. It had been settled by the English and Dutch in the late 1600. I loved history and wanted to know everything about this farmhouse.

One day I would research our farm and find out who Seymour might be. I saw an ad in the paper that read: "Come have dinner with a ghost."

The Lambertville Inn in Lambertville, New Jersey, was having a dinner. Guests were invited to dine with a ghost. Just how you conjure up a ghost while having dinner, I wanted to find out.

It took a while to talk Ray into this, but he finally agreed. It was a private dining room where we ate dinner, and the surroundings were beautiful. We were told of the inn's early history. It had been built in the 1700s and had always been an inn.

After dinner, we moved to another room, and I estimated that there were about thirty people there. We had a speaker, who told us about the many ghosts that still haunted the inn.

There were always guests telling the staff of their experiences and the things that they had witnessed after spending the night. And the staff had many stories of their own. When the speaker had finished, he asked who else would like to share their own ghost stories, if they had any. And much to my surprise, one by one, people started to talk about their experiences.

One woman had a rocker in her bedroom that had been in their family for generations.

She awoke from sleep one night and found it rocking by itself. She had just buried her mother and was sure it was her mother let-

94

ting her know that she was okay. She wasn't afraid and slowly fell back to sleep, watching it rock back and forth with a feeling of comfort that her mom was still with her. Nothing else ever happened. It was just that one night.

There were several people who had experiences that they were willing to share with everyone there that evening. There were the usual stories of doors that wouldn't stay shut or the opposite, doors that would not stay open. They spoke of lights that went off or on, and I listened with great interest. Every time someone had finished speaking, I would raise my hand only to have Ray push it down. About the third time I tried to raise my hand, Ray held my hand for the rest of the evening. He was not going to let me talk.

I was amazed at each of the stories, but one thing stood out. Everyone who spoke that evening had one thing happen they could not explain. I, on the other hand, was sitting on the yellow pages of ghost events I could not explain. Our ghost was having a bloody good time with us and did not appear to be leaving anytime soon. I had suspected we might have a poltergeist; from what I had read, they were supposed to be the pranksters of all ghosts. They were the ones who were always trying to scare you.

I knew that there were times when Seymour had done a damn good job of it. Young Ray and I had both had episodes where we had waited outside the house until someone came home. There had also been the time we had our backs to the wall as we came down a staircase.

I was always looking into some kind of explanation of what we might be dealing with. I really missed a golden opportunity to find out more about Seymour when the following guest came to visit one day on the farm.

I was working in the office now full-time. The second floor of the barn was now turned into office space.

There was Ray's office, and my office was right next to his. There was a large room that was a stockroom with two desks so when the men returned from their jobs, they could fill out their work orders for the day. It was lunchtime, and I was going over to the house for a sandwich. As I walked across the driveway to the house, a car pulled around the circle and stopped. I walked over to them and asked the driver if I could be of help.

A very handsome, distinguished-looking gentleman asked, "Are you the young lady of this beautiful home?"

Oh, and did I mention how charming he was?

When I answered yes, he introduced himself as Harry Snellenberg.

It was *the* Harry Snellenberg!

He had been the owner of this farm in the forties and fifties. They had been the prominent family who owned the farm when it had been a beautiful estate, and for the first few years, people would always refer to it as the old Snellenberg place. They implied that it would never be as beautiful as it had once been when it belonged to this family in the fifties.

Although I had not heard this for some time, would the work we had done meet his expectation? He was charming. He told me how his daughter after her visit had told him of the massive renovation that we had undertaken when she had visited a few years ago. Of course, I invited them in. He was with his wife and another couple, whom he introduced as friends.

They had heard about the farm for years from Harry and had wanted to see it. They were driving up to New Hope for lunch and had decided to stop. I assured him he was very welcome. I showed the four of them through the whole house as I always kept it in mint condition, even the bedrooms. I always made the beds every day and never asked my sons as they did plenty of work around the house. They were expected to keep their rooms neat.

I really believed Mr. Snellenberg loved what we had done. He was full of compliments.

We were still upstairs when Mrs. Snellenberg touched my arm and asked with a chuckle, "Are there any ghosts?"

As I stood there wondering what to say, their friends spoke, breaking the silence. I had been caught by surprise. Of course, I should have realized that he, Seymour, must have been around for all the other owners as well. I was sure Mrs. Snellenberg was disappointed as I never replied to her question, and I would always be sorry I did not answer her. I should have asked, "What stories do you have? And I'll tell you mine!"

What was Seymour up to forty-some years ago? Mrs. Snellenberg was the second Mrs. Snellenberg as he had been divorced after moving from the farm. This was according to his daughter when she had come to visit. This Mrs. Snellenberg would not have lived here and must have heard stories about the farm.

Life is made up of moments, and this moment was lost to me. I would have loved to know what Seymour had been up to back then. Of course, I shared all the stories of when we were renovating and how we endured all the stories of the famous Snellenbergs and how it was once a beautiful estate. He interrupted, assuring me that we had succeeded in returning it to its former glory.

I know that he must have been surprised as the home he lived in was a white plaster farmhouse and now it was all stone. I was sure he was pleased to see what had been under all that white plaster for years. It was like going back in history. We had also changed the driveway, and now the back of the house was the front of the house, as it had once been two hundred years ago. I believed he liked what he saw, and I could not have been happier.

They said their good-byes, and I watched them leave.

Now I could say I had met *the* Snellenbergs and had their seal of approval.

CHAPTER TWENTY-TWO

It was becoming increasingly hard to keep up the house as I liked to keep it.

Everyone knew that we had been restoring this two-hundred-year-old farm, and people were naturally curious. When someone stopped to visit for whatever reason, I would always ask if they would like to see the house. I really felt more like a curator of a museum. I enjoyed sharing what little I knew about the history of this wonderful old farm. I felt honored to be living here in the memories of so many other families from the past.

But I was not wonder woman.

Keeping this farmhouse immaculate was a lot of work, and working full-time was becoming impossible. Ray wanted me in the office by eight thirty. I never realized how hard it would be to maintain my home the way I wanted it kept and also work full-time.

This was how Sara came to live with us. I hired her to be a full-time housekeeper. No, we were not filthy rich. I was willing to give up most of my pay to have a housekeeper. I loved it. She would be with us for the next seven years. I had no intention of ever mentioning Seymour to Sara. We all agreed to say nothing. I was sure she would not want to work here if she knew.

Of course, Seymour made no such promise. I came over to the house one afternoon for lunch to find Sara in a mood. I could see she was annoyed. This was not at all like her.

I finally had to ask, "What's wrong?"

And she answered quickly. "I think your boys are playing jokes on me. I make the beds in the morning and straighten up their rooms. Then I am finished with that room. When I carry up the clean wash to be put away, I find the beds have been messed and I have to straighten them up again. I am only doing these beds once! I would appreciate it if you would tell them that. I don't like to complain, but it's really annoying. I never see them in the house, so they must come in another door just for the purpose of teasing me."

"Oh," I said, not knowing what else to say. My mind was racing. What if I told her and she was frightened and wouldn't want to stay? I would be hanging on her legs, crying for her not to leave as she dragged me across the floor. This was what I imagined in my mind. I was very fussy about my home, and she was perfect. She did a wonderful job. I could not lose her. If I didn't say anything about the unusual things that went on in the house, then she might grab one of the kids. They would surely tell her about Seymour. And they might say a whole lot more, like how he liked to scare us.

Oh, where do I start?

"Sara, I have been meaning to tell you something. Sometimes you might have some strange things that happen and it's hard to explain."

"Like what?" she asked.

"Well, like beds that sometimes get messed up when they were just made. I don't think it's the kids. You see, there have been times that things have happened, and there is no explanation. This seems to be one of them." I now had her attention. "You see this exact same thing often happened to my sister-in-law when she lived here. She would make her bed and, after her shower, would find it messed like someone had just laid down on it."

"Yeah," said Sara, "that's just what happens to me. It's like someone has just laid down to take a nap."

I went on to say, if you said aloud "that you're not going to put up with this and to stop it now" I don't believe it would happen again. It has worked for me."

Sara was now staring at me. There was silence between us as I held my breath.

A smile crossed her face, she said, "You've got to be kidding."

"I know it's hard to believe. I have lived here now for almost four years, and I still have trouble believing any of it. I know that it's not the kids. I have found that if you're angry and tell whatever it is to stop, it works."

Sara sat for a minute and said, "That would explain a lot of things. Once the bathroom door was locked, and I couldn't get in to clean it. I thought one of the boys was in there, but they said nothing when I asked who was in there. I have been blaming the boys for a lot of things. Well, I feel better now, knowing the boys have not been behind any of this. They are always so nice to me. I could not understand the change in their character. They are so nice to my face and then act like little demons in the house when I am alone."

"*Oh*, Sara, Please let's not use the word *demons*. I don't like the sound of that."

Sara asked, "We are talking about ghosts, aren't we?"

"Yes, but I think there is only one—at least most of the time."

I was happy that Sara seemed to be okay with our conversation.

It could really take a while before you'd begin to believe in ghosts. I was still trying to come up with practical or more scientific explanations. Sara was about five feet nine inches and was big-boned. She was not heavy but was a large woman. I think she could have handled anyone that might give her trouble. I couldn't believe anyone would want to give her trouble. She just might be the one to straighten out Seymour.

I asked, "Then you're okay with this?"

"Yes," she answered. "I have never known what to think about ghosts. I never had any experience with anything like this. But now that I know, I will let him know not to mess with me. I am only cleaning up once."

Sara went on as the days passed with her stories of doors that would not stay closed, a common thing in this house, and how each time she made the beds she told him, "Don't mess this up," in a threatening voice. So far, it was working.

One day, while in the kitchen, Sara heard me calling her from what she thought sounded like the porch. Young Ray was in the house downstairs, coming from the library, and he also heard me calling at the same time. Sara came out from the dining room door to where I was standing on the porch and asked me what I wanted. A second later, young Ray opened the door from the living room and asked me if I was calling him.

When I answered no to both of them, that I had not called anyone, we all looked at one another and laughed. That was how we handled these moments.

Sara only wanted to know how she would know the difference. I assured her if I needed her, I would come into the room and talk to her. I would not call her from a distance.

I thought about this for a while. Two people at the same time had heard what they thought was me calling them. Was this a woman's voice, and was she living here? Young Ray was sure it was me calling him down to a party on the day he was alone.

It appeared we had quite a variety of guests. I still felt there was one dominant figure that was the main character in this cast. He was the one that liked to play games.

We still had on occasion the gentleman who liked to smoke a pipe in the dining room. We had the children in the small bedroom who giggled the night Ray and I went in the room, seeking Seymour. And last we had the prankster who liked to scare us. Could there be a woman in this cast of characters, or could this all be explained by one entity?

One day I invited our closest neighbors, the Sollys, over to show them what we had done with the farmhouse. They had remembered what it had looked like when the Snellenbergs had owned it. They sold food that was grown on their land. Barbara would often ask how the renovations were coming. When I finished showing them the house and we were standing at the main staircase in the center hall, she asked me if I had ever been told that a man's body had been found at the bottom of this center hall staircase.

"No," I answered. "When did this happen?"

"It was in 1921, and they could not determine how he died," she answered.

I wondered, *Could this be our gentleman who likes to smoke his pipe in the dining room?*

I did not mention our pipe smoker to our neighbor. I did, however, make a resolution to find out who had lived in this house. It would still be some time before I would start this search, but I was going to find out who they were—the whole lot of them.

CHAPTER TWENTY-THREE

As time passed, I grew very fond of Sara. She had a kind heart. There were a great many animals that would pass through our home, all having been rescued. We all learned so many things from the animals that came into our lives. It was a journey of growth, and Sara too was part of this journey.

Apparently, I was the only farm that kept dry food out in my barn for my two cats, along with fresh water. Both my cats had been spayed and neutered. They had been given to me from the barn where I had boarded my horse. They loved each other. I had assured my friend that I would take good care of them. I never dreamed that all the neighboring farms that had barn cats would learn of the barn that kept food out all day, every day, and would just stop by. I would be told that farmers don't believe in feeding barn cats. They thought the cats would not want to catch rats or mice. Of course, I disagreed. To chase and catch rats or mice was their source of play. Cats must be fed to keep them healthy. Rats or mice should not be their diet. This would subject them to disease. A good diet kept them healthy and enjoying their sport.

I quickly learned that animals could and did talk to one another. Before long, I had quite a few cats. During the time we would live there, over the course of years, I had fifty-plus cats spayed and neutered. In the beginning, we were having our share of kittens, all of which I did a good job of finding homes.

I say here that no one should allow a cat to have kittens. There are too many people who feel cats are disposal animals. They do not realize how many litters each female can have in one year. They feel that cats can survive on their own. It's not true. They need shelter from the cold and the elements as well as from predators, not to mention good food and fresh water.

The second year we were there, I had two cats come from another barn and have their babies in our barn. While returning to their farm across the road, both mothers were hit and killed by a car. That was the year I spent my summer feeding twelve baby kittens. I swore I would never let this happen again. Most of the cats that I was having fixed were from area farms. All of mine had been fixed. I kept waiting to hear from the local farmers that they had no kittens this year, then I would know I was finished.

One day while the kids were cutting the grass, Mark came running around to my office in the barn. He was yelling he had just found a baby raccoon. He had thought it was a rock. He bent down to pick it up so as not to run over the rock with the mower. It looked like a round stone in the palm of your hand. It was still warm. I asked him to take it back to the very place he had found it and to watch from a distance to see if its mom would come back for it. He did exactly that, but the mom never returned.

I'd had a great many experiences having done just that. Often, the mother would return, but you must keep vigil so no predator would take them for food. I had a mother bird return for her baby one day.

I rescued a baby bird just before my cats were thinking he might be lunch. He must have been learning how to fly. I kept him overnight, and the next morning, I cradled the fragile baby bird in my hand as I put him on our post and rail fence. I watched from my window. He could not fly yet. It was heartwarming to hear him call and watch his mom fly to him. She coaxed him all the way down the fence line, inch by inch, until she reached a very thick lilac bush, and there they both disappeared. Someone could have given me a winning lottery ticket that day, and I wouldn't have traded it for that moment.

I think I had just witnessed what Albert Einstein had been quoted as saying:

Look deep into Nature
And then you will understand
Everything Better

Sara was always making formula KMR for the kittens or Espalac for our new baby raccoon, now named Taddy. He was as small as a tadpole, and his name later became Taddy. It was not uncommon to find Sara holding Taddy if he was crying like you would a baby. Among the kittens that I had raised that summer, there was one kitten in particular that would continue to come over from the barn to the house. I happened to be looking out the window of my office when I noticed this tiny kitten sitting by the kitchen door. Sara opened the door and scooped her up and disappeared into the kitchen.

I spotted Sara's little kitten later with her full round belly, heading back to the barn, I guess, for her nap.

Yes, Sara fit right in with the rest of us.

CHAPTER TWENTY-FOUR

W e were always losing tools when we were renovating the farm-house. We never really thought anything about it. We would just go and buy another one. Ray was always blaming the boys and telling them they would have to be more careful. I could not understand it. We always cleaned up after our work and put all the tools away. We could not have been more careful.

When we were finished renovating the farmhouse, Ray was shocked to find he had fifteen hammers. We had, at that time, no idea that things might disappear all by themselves. It wasn't until after we had moved in the main house that we began to take notice. It was small things, like a book that someone needed for school or jewelry that I wanted to wear that day. I began to ask for it back. I started it as a joke, but before long, I realized it worked.

One night in the kitchen, Ray was making a sandwich, and he could not find the milk. He had taken it out of the refrigerator and put it on the counter. I had watched him do this. We were busy talking, and when he reached for the milk, he asked me what I had done with it.

"Nothing," I answered, "you must have moved it."

He said, "No, I didn't."

"Then get something else to drink," I said.

"No, I want the milk," said Ray. It was then I told Ray what I had been doing when I could not find something and asked him to ask for the milk back.

"That is ridiculous! I am not about to ask for it back. It's right here somewhere. We just need to look."

Ray and I spent the next half hour looking for the milk. We looked in the refrigerator. We checked all the counters and checked the cabinets. We even looked in the laundry room just in case we carried it out there. He was sure I must have carried it off.

After thirty minutes or more, I finally begged Ray, "Just ask for it back!"

He did reluctantly, and as we turned around, it was right in front of us in the sink. Now, I know that you're thinking we must have missed this, but we didn't.

The following story best illustrates the strange events that would happen and why I asked for everything lost to be returned!

I ask you, have you ever wrapped a gift and the person you gave it to opened an empty box? This is exactly what happened to me one Christmas.

I had become very good friends with a wildlife rehabilitator named Jeanne. We had met over our raccoon, Taddy. She had a group of friends that helped her care for orphaned animals. I was now helping when she had some orphaned raccoons. She introduced me to two young girls that worked for our local vet. They would often stop by. We liked to share stories of the animals we had cared for, or they would assist me with some new orphan. They were twins, and Jeanne would often refer to them as the girls.

They were going off to college in the fall. I knew I would see them during the holidays. I bought each one a gold necklace. It was a leaf that had been gold dipped. I wrapped each necklace in a separate box, and when they visited during the holidays, I gave them their gifts. I told them to open them on Christmas morning.

I never gave this another thought. Just after Christmas, Jeanne called and told me that Stephanie had opened an empty box. Stacey had opened her gift and was wearing her necklace, but Stephanie's box was empty. I told Jeanne that this had never happened to me before. She explained that the girls would never have said anything to me and had asked Jeanne not to say anything. Of course, I assured her I would look for it or that I would buy her another one if I could not find it. I looked through all the wrapping paper but to no avail.

During the holidays, I always put out my Anne Lee dolls. They were collectibles. After the holidays, I would store them in the closet in the library that had ceiling-to-floor shelves. I would wash all the shelves and line the shelves with white tissue paper. I then put the dolls on the shelves from top to bottom. The closet was now filled with Anna Lee dolls with their smiling faces looking out at you. It was funny to open up the closet and see them staring at you. I also kept a plastic container under the bottom shelf and stored wrapping paper in there. I kept Christmas and birthday paper in this closet.

I never found the necklace, and I had looked everywhere. I had intended to purchase another one for Stephanie, but life often got in the way of our best intentions. I would not see Stephanie until six months later when one night I had an emergency. After all this time, I had forgotten all about the missing necklace.

It was the summer, and I was on my way home from the feed mill. It was my favorite place to shop. I would pick out treats for the horses, dogs, and cats. As I drove up to my farm, there was something in the road. I had to drive over it as I had traffic on the other side of the road and cars right behind me. I was careful to make sure that it was between my tires so I would not run over it. Just as I drove over it, I saw it was one of my barn cats, and he had just lifted his head. I put on the brakes as I turned into our driveway. I was now screaming as I ran back toward his body still lying in the street.

I must have stopped the traffic, but didn't even remember doing so. All I wanted was to reach him before another car ran over him. He was lying still. I gently lifted his body and quickly carried him to the house. I knew the girls were still working for our local vet during the summer. However, I knew the office would be closed now. It was early Friday evening. I would not be able to get my cat to the vet. I called the girls' home, and their mother said she would call Stephanie, who was on a date.

Stephanie left her date and opened the vet's office. She came to my home with an IV and administered an IV of saline solution. She explained this would help to keep my cat from going into shock. They were both in school to be vets. I was so grateful she was able to come over and help me. The next morning, my cat, now fully awake, was upset to find himself in my kitchen, especially with the dogs. You would have thought I was the one who had hit him in the head. He must have had a concussion, but he was definitely feeling better. I let him out, and the way he ran back to the barn, I was sure he had stories to tell all his friends.

It was July; I remember this because it was my husband's birthday. I needed wrapping paper for my husband's gift. I was telling Sara all about what had happened last night. I left the kitchen and looked back, asking Sara to remind me to buy Stephanie a gift for her kindness.

I went to the library, and as I opened the door to the closet (this was the closet that held the Anna Lee dolls and the wrapping paper that was stored in a box under the bottom shelf), I gasped. There straight in front of me, at eye level, stretched out as if on display, lying on the white tissue paper, was the necklace. It was the gold necklace that Stephanie never received at Christmas.

Not a minute had passed since I had asked Sara to remind me to buy Stephanie a gift.

I ran through the house, screaming for Sara. I wanted to know if Sara could have found this necklace and placed it there on the shelf. Of course, Sara had never seen this necklace before. She remarked how it looked like it had been staged. I agreed. This for me was one of the strangest events that ever happened. It was right up there with the strange evening when Ray and I had been fighting.

At this point, what else could I believe? Seymour had heard me and returned Stephanie's necklace. It had been Stephanie who opened the empty box that Christmas morning.

CHAPTER TWENTY-FIVE

The boys were out riding their dirt bikes one Saturday afternoon. Mike came running around the house and came in to tell me that some animal was under the corn crib. They could hear it growling. I assured him that we had no dangerous animals in the area we lived in. We had a lot of deer in our area, and I knew they didn't growl.

I told him I would check it out. I walked around the barn with a bowl of dog food. I stopped outside the corn crib. The boys were gone, but I could hear their bikes from a distance. I called softly, thinking it might be a dog or a feral cat; they could growl. I stooped down to look under the corn crib but saw nothing. Then suddenly, something moved. I could not make it out. The area under the corn crib was not that large an area.

It could not be a very big animal. I set the bowl down and stood back. I called again in a very soothing voice. A nose appeared but would not move any further. I was now sure it was a dog. I walked back for a bowl of water, and when I returned, the food was gone. There was no sign of a dog anywhere.

This might take a few days, I thought. He was obviously very frightened.

I told the boys during dinner that I thought it was a dog.

Ray was quick to say, "We don't need any more animals. We have two great dogs. We don't need any more!"

We didn't mention it again, but the next morning, I was out back of the barn with a bowl of dog food. This time when I called softly, a head appeared. I could hear her whining. I thought it might be a girl. I could now see her soft brown eyes were pleading. I knew she wanted to come out to me. I set the bowl of food down where I was standing and backed a short distance away. I have met timid dogs before, but I was quite sure she had suffered abuse. I continued to encourage her to come out.

It seemed like forever, but finally a cream-colored shepherd crawled out from under her hiding place. She was dirty but otherwise looked to be okay. She belly-crawled to the food bowl, crying and whining as she inched closer. I continued to talk to her, but the moment I moved toward her, she was gone. She had disappeared into the cornfield. I left the food bowl and fresh water. I suspected it would take some time to win her trust; I was wrong.

That same day, late in the afternoon, a man walked up the back road where I was checking the food bowl and said, "I think I have just hit your dog. He's lying on the road, hurt."

Just then Ray appeared and said, "Our dogs are fine. I just left them in the house."

The man described a cream-colored dog, and I gasped, "Ray, get a blanket. We must get her off the road."

Ray went for a blanket. The cars moved around us while we gently lifted her up from the road. I thanked the driver for his kindness. He could have driven off and left her to die. She would have surely been hit by another car. We carried her to my car. She was whining the whole time but couldn't move. We carefully slid the blanket on to the backseat. She was so good the whole time. On our way to the vet, I had to endure a lecture.

"Rob," he started, "there comes a time when we must be practical. She isn't our dog. She is going to require a lot of care—not to mention the costs involved. She might not be able to be saved."

I answered, "We'll let the vet tell us what her injuries are. Then we'll make a decision."

This seemed to calm Ray as we carried her into the vet's office, explaining we had an emergency. The nurse ushered us back to a room. We lifted her onto the table. This was the first time I was so close to her face. I could have kissed her. She was really beautiful. I kept talking to her. I wanted her to know she had nothing to fear.

The vet walked in, and at that moment, Ray said, "She's not our dog. She was hit on the road in front of our farm."

I told the vet I wanted to know what her injuries were. Ray agreed we would wait for the vet's prognosis. Of course, he had to take x-rays. There were no internal injuries, but her hip and pelvic bones were crushed. He did not have the expertise to do the surgery. She needed a specialist; he said he knew of such an expert. He was only two hours away in New York.

By the way Ray rolled his eyes back in his head, I thought he might be having a stroke.

Ray continued telling me to be practical and telling the vet she was not our dog while the vet continued giving me directions to the orthopedic surgeon, never once looking at Ray. Our vet called the surgeon to explain in detail the extent of her injuries and assure him we were on our way. The surgeon agreed to wait. On the trip up to the surgeon's office, Ray kept telling me I needed to be realistic. I could not continue to save every animal that crossed my path.

I answered, "She has no internal injuries, and once she has this operation, she would be as good as new." Ray did not even hear me, so I sat quietly while Ray carried on about what the cost of this operation might be. I could not have counted the number of times Ray told me she was not our dog. I got it!

What he didn't know was that she was going to be our dog. I knew this yesterday the first day I saw her behind our barn. We arrived at the surgeon's office and carried her in. She was now talking to us. There were soft sounds coming from this lovely blond-haired dog. I was sure she had been dumped. How long had she been on her own, I had no way of knowing.

The surgeon was even better at ignoring Ray's protests than our vet. I don't think the vet even looked in Ray's direction until Ray repeated the price he had just quoted.

"Yes, it will cost you two thousand dollars for this operation," the vet repeated.

Again, Ray's eyes rolled back in his head.

What was going on with him? I thought. The doctor looked back at me and continued to inform me as to how long she would have to stay. I don't believe he ever looked back at Ray again.

Ray's voice was even louder as he stated, "But you don't understand, Doc. She's not our dog!"

Ray and I drove home in silence. Finally, perhaps now, he understood.

We brought our dog home after a week with the specialist. Ray now referred to her as our six-million-dollar dog. We could not keep her with the other dogs as she had not even met them yet. And she needed time to recover. The vet had asked that we keep her quiet.

We also had another problem as I explained to the vet. He said it was called submissive behavior. Wolves did it when one lone wolf was entering a new pack. She would lie on her back with her tail tucked between her legs. When you approached her, she would wag her tail and sprayed you with urine. Her tail was tucked so tightly between her legs, it acted as a fan. This was dog language that she was surrendering herself to you. You could do what you wanted with her, and she would submit to it.

She wanted to be accepted and be part of the pack. I asked the vet if we could keep her in a clean box stall with fresh bedding while she recovered. He instructed me how to cure this problem. When I let her out each morning, I was not to talk or praise her at all.

"When she is still and quiet and sitting by your side, only then can you pat her head," he explained. This way, she would learn that she had to remain quiet and calm before she could get what she craved most—affection. She learned after only three days, and this was testament to how smart she was.

I have never met a stupid dog, only a stupid owner.

She now sat quietly. She had stopped falling on her back and peeing. Oh, what trauma had she experienced in her young life? According to the vet, she was just a year old, barely. When she finally was able to meet Max and Sandra, we had no problem.

Sandra, of course, did not like her. Sandra, being a little lady, would charge her only when no one was around. Sandra had had Max all to herself. She did not like the attention he was paying to this new girl. But the new dog took it in stride. Ray had been calling her the terror dog. We needed a better name. We came up with *Tara*. It would replace *Terror*.

She was in the house by the end of the month with her own new cushion to lie on. She was now part of the pack, and I couldn't be happier.

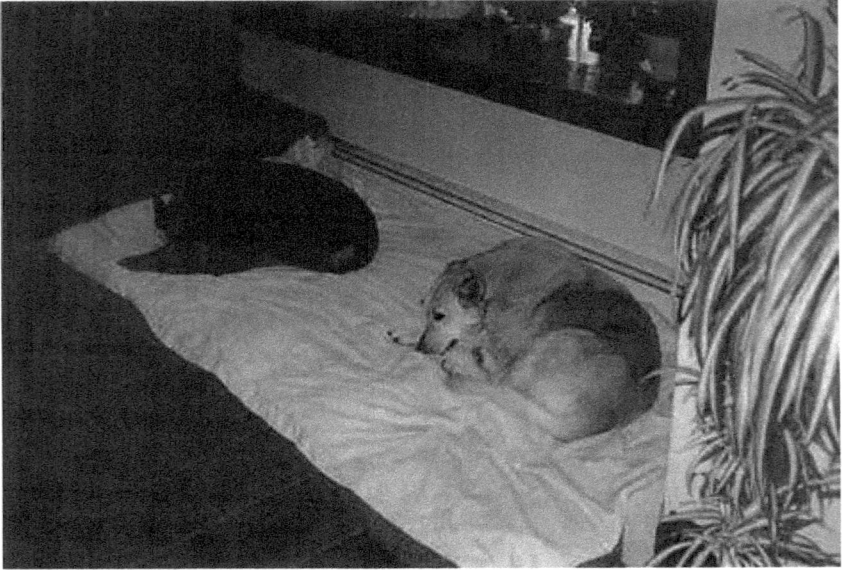

CHAPTER TWENTY-SIX

I now had three large dogs, and in addition to protection, perhaps one or all of them might spot Seymour. He had not played with the basement door since the night that we had been laughing at him. I had often wondered if dogs could see things that we couldn't. Their sense of smell was so strong that perhaps they could locate Seymour and the rest of our residents.

Ray, our eldest son, was now driving and would never come home when no one else was there. If no one was home, he would go back to the house of his girlfriend, Lisa. He would ask to stay there. It was a little easier now with the dogs, but they slept in the kitchen. I had wanted them to sleep upstairs with the rest of us.

But Ray insisted, "With this many dogs in the house, we would have traffic jams in the hallway."

"We only have three dogs," I insisted.

That's how Ray, said no; it was always with humor.

"But the dogs would not be of much help throughout the rest of the house if they were only allowed in the kitchen," I argued. Of course, I was not sure that even the dogs could have helped anyone with the unforeseen. Still, having dogs in the house, you'd never feel like you were alone; they give you such comfort.

There were no cars in the driveway when young Ray pulled in and drove around the circle on that night. Michael was due back from his trip to Ohio. He was sure that he had a ride and would have been dropped off. Little Mike's first love had moved to Ohio with her family, and we had let him fly out to visit her. Young Ray was aware of this and figured his brother would be home by now. As Ray walked through the house and climbed the stairs, he felt that familiar feeling of being watched.

He slowly walked down the hallway, and he saw what he thought was Mike just ahead of him. He called out to him as he continued to follow what he thought was Mike.

Perhaps Mike had not heard him, so Ray walked into Mike's bedroom and continued down the hallway to our bedroom; it was there when he realized he was following a shadow. A shadow was leading him through the house, and he could not catch up with it. It was here when he realized no one was home. He was here alone. Yet there was someone else there with him. He had no trouble making a quick exit from the house. He never looked back as he raced to the back door. The dogs, he thought, would have to take care of themselves. They were on their own. I heard the whole story the next morning.

I had a terrible cold the following week. I sat in the kitchen, drinking hot tea in the hope I would feel better. I was enjoying sitting there with the dogs. We had a fire in the potbellied stove, and all the dogs were lying around on the floor as close as they could get without getting burned. Then I noticed Sandra was standing and facing the corner of the kitchen. There was nothing in the corner of the room—at least nothing I could see. But here was Sandra staring into the corner and wagging her tail. She was acting as if someone was talking to her. I wondered who she might be looking at.

I had always trusted a dog's instinct. If it was Seymour, then she liked him. Or could it be one of the children that Ray and I had heard one evening in the middle of the night. Whichever one of the spirits that I was quite sure was in our kitchen, our dog Sandra liked him. Who were they? I made up my mind on that night that I was going to take the time necessary to research all who had lived here, were still living here, and more importantly, why they did not want to leave.

The next morning, I called Phyllis, a dear friend, and asked her if she could meet me in the deed room of the courthouse. Phyllis worked in the courthouse and said she was happy to help me get started. I drove to the courthouse. I was thinking of Phyllis as I drove. We had been friends since we were children. And I valued her friendship. That day I needed her help just to show me how to trace the deeds of all who had owned this property. I needed to go back to the beginning when it all started.

"I'm coming for you, Seymour," I said softly and smiled at the thought.

CHAPTER TWENTY-SEVEN

P hyllis had moved into the cottage after we had moved out of our cottage a.k.a. pool house. She had asked if she could move in for several months. Of course, I said yes. She was moving back to this area from Pt. Pleasant, New Jersey, and had not wanted to move in with her mom. She needed to look for a job and an apartment. Phyllis is like a sister to me. I lived with her and her family as a young girl off and on. I was happy to help. She did not stay too long, only a couple of months. I was disappointed when she moved so quickly. I had wondered if I had said anything that might have upset her!

I still had days of denial about Seymour, so why would I think that someone else might be experiencing anything? We were sitting in the deed room of the courthouse, and I had just finished telling her about young Ray and the shadow that he had followed down the hallway and through the house. It was now for the first time that Phyllis shared her story and the following event.

"Oh, Rob," she started. "I did not know how to tell you. I was afraid of what you might think. I know how hard you have all worked on restoring your farm, so how could I tell you I knew your house was haunted? At first, I started out thinking I was letting my fear get ahead of me. When I would pull into the driveway in the evening after work and realize that no one was home, my heart would sink. I had to make myself walk across the dark driveway to the cottage with dread. I would be shaking by the time I got out my keys to unlock the door. The feeling would not stop there. I always felt someone was there with me all the time. It would go away for a while when I turned on the TV. The sound of the TV gave me some comfort.

The finished pool house

Inside the pool house

"I have seen the shadow that young Ray was talking about from my bathroom many times when taking a shower. I know exactly what Ray saw that evening. The first time it happened, I called out, thinking maybe someone had come in not knowing I was there. I got out of the shower, wrapped a towel around me, and searched the cottage. I already knew I wouldn't find anyone. To make myself feel better, I would ask it to leave. It was worse when I couldn't sleep. I would lie awake with the bedroom door open. I would watch for any signs of anything moving. I was making plans to move out only days after I moved in. I am so sorry I didn't tell you before, but I kept telling myself that maybe I was imagining all this because it's so lonely out here. There are no houses anywhere around, and I didn't want you to think I was being silly."

"I really do understand," I said and proceeded to tell Phyllis some of the things that had happened to us from the time we had moved in. I was happy to know that it was not anything that I might have said. It was now that I remembered the electric mixer that had gone on in the middle of the night when we lived in the cottage. I told Phyllis about the mixer and said, "I never thought it was anything except a short in the circuit."

I thanked Phyllis for her help in the deed room as she needed to get back to the tax office, where she worked. She had helped me get started in tracing the deeds. I found it very interesting how each deed gave you a number from the deed before. I was going back in time with the many people who had lived in this house.

As I started this paper journey, the farm was already fifteen acres. We had bought ten acres and later added five acre tract of land. The size of the farm changed with the many owners. I was now looking at the deed from the Snellenburgs, and they did indeed get divorced. They transferred ownership of the farm for one dollar, and when they sold the property, they divided the land.

They sold a hundred acres off to a transportation company, and ten acres was sold with the house.

I wondered if anyone in the afterlife would be upset as their once-beloved farm was sold off in pieces. I learned why the daughter of Harry Snellenberg had said that everyone living on this farm got divorced. The next five deeds going back to 1921 were transferred in divorce. I wondered, *Could Seymour have been visiting their families during their struggles?*

It did appear that around circa 1921, 1926, and 1927, there were three owners whose heirs transferred the deed for one dollar. It appeared that three owners in a short time passed away, and ownership was transferred to their heirs. This coincides with the story about a man being found dead at the bottom of the center hall staircase in about 1921.

I wondered, *Did he smoke a pipe?*

There was a story here, I was quite sure, but I couldn't get sidetracked. I was looking for Seymour and our other houseguests.

I was now looking at the deed dated March 26, 1884, and the house was being sold by the heirs of John Scott. I remembered that name; it was on a tombstone we found in the barn. Oh, I had forgotten all about this story as it was not about a ghost but a grave site.

Chapter Twenty-Eight

W e had been in the house for a few years now, but we were still not finished. Ray was not happy if he did not have a project going. We did not start on the barn until the house was finished. The wing of the barn had been rebuilt. We now had our business here and were ready to finish the stalls. We started in the small room that was adjacent to the stall area. This would be the tack room when it was done. We never understood why the floor was uneven. We used this room as a maintenance shop. When you walked in, it was like walking on small hills.

The dirt floor was hard red clay, but we never gave it a thought as to why it was so much higher than the stall area. The floor was irregular and would have to be dug out to make it even with the rest of the floor. We needed to get it ready to pour for a concrete floor.

We were all here digging in this small room next to the main barn. It was a beautiful evening when a shovel that young Ray was digging with hit something hard. The entire time we had renovated the farm, we had never found anything of historic value—until now. We all looked at each other and joked that we had found the buried treasure that we had been looking for, and of course, Ray Sr. took over. He was the first to use his hand and brush back the dirt.

We were all hoping to uncover a treasure chest. We all gasped when Ray said, "It's a tombstone."

We had uncovered a headstone lying face up. Someone was buried here.

Ray picked up the tombstone—it was broken in half—and read the following inscription:

In Memory Of Mary Scott
Died 10th Month 26 Day 1845
Lived 55 years 5 Months

"Why would she be buried in the barn?" I asked.

Ray guessed that at one time, this area was outside of the original barn and could have been a small family grave site. We were all thinking the same thing. Could there be more people buried here just below our feet? We discussed whether we should continue digging any further, but we were all in agreement that it would be sacrilegious to disturb this resting site. We already had our share of spirits in the house and were not looking for any more. Ray asked Mark to get our camera so we could take a picture of it exactly where we had found it.

It was then that we realized we had only the top half of the tombstone. Ray looked at the boys, and by the look on all their faces at that exact moment, they knew where the other half of the marble was. When we had first bought the farm, there was a beautiful piece of marble sitting on the dirt under a spigot in the paddock area alongside a stall door where a bowl of water was placed for the dog and cats. It kept the area from turning into mud when we filled the water bowl. We had used the broken piece of marble in a walk that we had laid alongside the barn. We now laid the broken headstone down on the walkway, matched it to the lower piece of marble. It was a perfect fit.

We were quite sure that Mary was buried there in the barn. We did not want to disturb the grave site. It may have been a small graveyard, and there might be others down there. It would be wrong to disturb this area.

It was possible that this part of the barn might have been added later and built over this grave site. We decided that they would remain there forever. I did not want to call anyone in like the historical society. I did not feel we had the right to change their location as this was where they chose to be buried. Nor did I want to know who else might be down there. We all bowed our heads, and in prayer, we asked that they rest in peace. We continued to prepare the area for concrete.

Mary Scott's tombstone when we uncovered it.

The walkway on the side of the barn where we
had used the other half of the marble

Left to Right
Mark, Mike
and Ray

All this work and
they still had a
sense of humor

Ripping out
the stalls

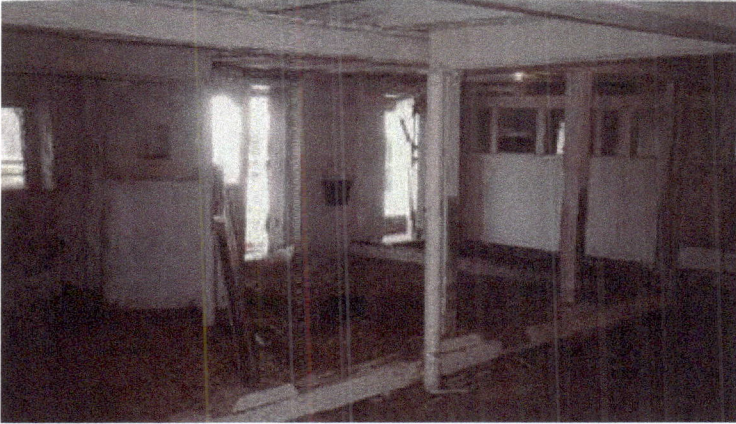

Before

During

In the beginning

Mark painting trim

Before

Before we started

Back of the barn was now finished but
still outbuildings to take down

The
Barn

← Before

After →

I painted
the huge
doors

← Before

After →

CHAPTER TWENTY-NINE

I had forgotten all about this until now when I was looking at the name on the deed.

There was something else here that was very confusing. We had also known that a woman named Mary Scott had lived, died, and was buried here, but the dates on the tombstone did not match the dates the property was owned by the Scott family.

When Mary Scott had died in March 1845, the property was owned by Silas Yerkes; her family would not own this property for another twenty-two years. Silas Yerkes bought the farm in April of 1830. Mary Scott died fifteen years later; she was buried there on the farm while Silas owned it. The Scott family would not buy the farm until April of 1867.

Silas would live here for thirty-nine years. Could she have worked for Silas? And why would the Scott family be the very next family to buy the farm? Did they do this because Mary was buried here? There are more questions here than answers. And just a thought—could Mary be the voice that everyone thought was me?

Over the course of weeks that led into months, I would slowly uncover the mystery of the farmhouse. I thought of myself as a sleuth, and my search would take me back into the early beginnings of the pioneers who literally settled this country. When Silas Yerkes bought the farmhouse, it was about 110 years old, and the appraiser who had appraised the farmhouse had noted it was old and in need of great repair. It would be Silas that would renovate the farmhouse and extended it to twice its size.

There was not a lot known about Silas or any mention of a wife.

Silas purchased the farmhouse of 109 acres from Richard Corson and his wife, Elizabeth (Kroesen) Corson. The deeds were on microfilm to preserve the documents. It was here when the name Kroesen was mentioned to the clerk who was helping me. She told me the Kroesen family had been early settlers of this area and that the historical society had five books that had been written on that family. She went on to say that when a farm was in the family for more than a hundred years, passed down from generation to generation, it was known as a century farm and that might be what we had.

I now took my search to the Spruance Library in Doylestown. They held all the historical documents from the area. The deeds had been traced back in history, but now it would be easier for a better understanding to start at the beginning and go forward and meet up with Silas Yerkes. I did not intend to write about history, but this was where I suspected I had uncovered the identity of Seymour.

Of course, everything started with William Penn. In 1684 he granted 2,000 acres to Arthur Cook, who granted to John Borden 1,000 acres of the said 2,000 acres and then, on December 15, 1720, deeded 500 acres to Derrick Krusen. (It's the same name, just spelled differently, which I will explain later, as there are many different spellings.) And on August 27, 1727, by deed of gift, he granted 250 acres to his son Francis Cruson. Francis Krusen will build two homes on this 250 acres. On this same document, there were two different spellings of the same person. Sons would often decide to spell their names differently from their fathers', or the clerks recording the deeds would spell what they thought or what it sounded like.

Anyone who had done research on our early settlers had found this, which made it harder to trace the same family. I was fortunate to have had all this hard work done for me by Frank King (Swain) of Fonthill, who in 1933 traced his family tree. He was a Kroesen. It was he that recorded the five books at the historical society on the Kroesen family. Seymour was a Kroesen—or so I believed.

The Kroesens were Dutch. They sailed from Holland in 1662 and settled in Staten Island. Their name at that time was spelled *Kroeson*. Along with the name came the many different spellings of their last names. It became even more difficult to research when they would name their children's first names after mothers, fathers, aunts, uncles, and cousins.

Our story follows four Derrick Kroesens.

Derrick number one was born in Staten Island about 1663. He brought his children to Bucks County about 1710. Derrick was the father of Francis. It was Francis who built his first home, and it was the home being researched on the 250 acres given to him by his father. It was not deeded to him legally until the traveling court circuit judge came to that area and recorded all transactions of deeded properties. Francis's home was deeded to him in 1727, about seven years after he had lived there.

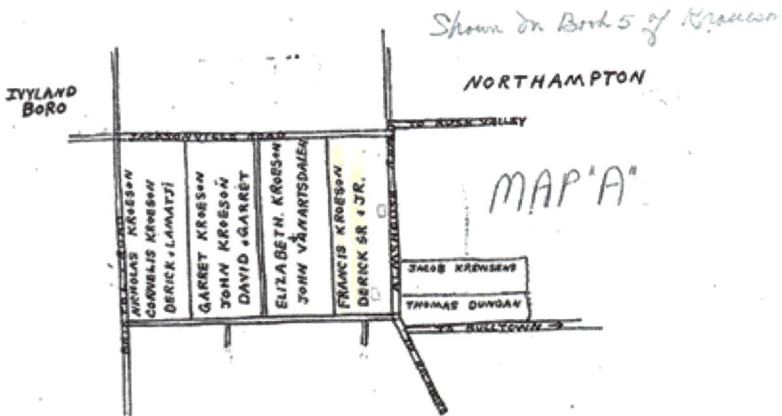

This drawing was copied from a book about the Kroesen family, showing how Derrick and Elizabeth divided the land among their children. On the lot marked "Francis" two homes were built. At this time, around 1720, the family was farming one thousand acres.

Francis built his home in 1720 or earlier as his father held a mortgage on this land in 1715, and Francis married his wife, Elizabeth Van De Grift, in 1716. Francis and his wife, Elizabeth, lived together and had three children. The oldest was a son named Derrick, after his grandfather.

On December 11, 1722, Francis, and the forty other settlers now living on lands adjacent of Southampton petitioned the Quarter Sessions Court for a new township that it would no longer be lands north of Southampton along with twenty-one other signers. On December 14, 1722, the name Northampton was adopted.

Francis gave his name as both resident and farmer of Northampton.

This was how townships were formed. For the next nineteen years, Francis lived on and farmed this land. Francis then sold his farm to his cousin in 1739, George Neefiers. He was also a Kroesen by marriage. George Neefiers died in 1756, and the farm was inherited by his son, Peter.

Francis was at the time living in New Castle, Delaware, with his wife's family, and he died a few weeks after his cousin George. On November 10, 1756, Derrick number two, Francis's son, bought back from his cousin Peter his father's home and the home of his childhood.

Derrick number two lived with his wife, Mary, and their eight children, one of which was named Derrick. He would later inherit the farm of his grandfather and father. He would be Derrick number three. He also had a brother who was afflicted. The father Derrick bought a farm across the road, and that farm was inherited by their brother Jacob.

Derrick number two was providing for his son Nicholas. He expressed in his will that Nicholas should live with both Derrick and Jacob and be cared for and supported in food and drink, washing, and apparel during his natural lifetime. This was his wish as stated in his will in February 18, 1789. He appeared to be a kind man as in his will, he stated his wishes in "loving affection" for his children. It did not state what Nick's affliction was, but I wondered, perhaps Nicholas liked to play games and just never stopped.

Derrick number three was born just four years after Derrick (son of Francis) bought back his father's farm; Derrick number three was born on November 14, 1760. He was the second son; Jacob was the first. These two brothers looked after Nicholas.

Derrick number three is grandson to Francis, and he married Elizabeth (Vansant). They had seven children. Mary, their first child, died at age two. They had a little girl born two years later who would also be named Mary. Then followed Charles, Elizabeth, Charity, James, and lastly, Jane.

In the last will and testament of Derrick number three, in the division of real estate, James was to have his father's estate. Charles took the second property. This was the first mention of a second property. It was my belief that both properties were built around the same time. They were a large family of brothers, sisters, and cousins and were farming a thousand acres.

It was here that the story took a strange twist. Charles did not live to see his father's estate settled. After only six months, he died at age thirty-four on September 1824. He left two children—Derrick C., and Elizabeth. Derrick C., or Derrick number four, died at age thirteen years and six weeks—just six weeks following his father's death. It was here during my research that I went to Orphans' Court to check further on Derrick C. It was here that I learned that the grandmother of Derrick cried foul play and petitioned the courts to withhold the estate from going to the next heir, which would have been his mother, Ann. The grandmother at this time had just lost her son six weeks earlier and now her grandson was dead.

But there was no mention of this in the five books of the Kroesen family on record at Spruance Library in Doylestown. The estate was then left to the sole surviving heir, Anne the widow of Charles. She later married Edward Vannuxem. If Derrick C. died of natural causes, then why would the grandmother declare in the courts that there was foul play? This would have been the son of Charles who had died. It would have been Charles who would have lived and grown up in the other house on the property. Derrick C. would have been his father's heir upon his father's death.

The question is, can a ghost occupy a house that he did not live in, or was he killed in this house that was referred to all the time in the wills as the "mansion house" and the one being researched?

Could there have been a deadly accident in which this young boy was killed and the grandmother, so grief-stricken, petitioned the courts and implied that her grandson's death was mysterious?

Only questions, but no answers. I did try to research this further, but the earliest names were given often to aunts, uncles, and cousins. "Elizabeth" and "Derrick" were used so often that there could be as many as ten or more in the same family.

I have for some time suspected that Seymour might be a child. A young boy's voice is still high at age thirteen and could be the voice that everyone heard and thought was mine. He might be all the entities in the house—*only* him!

Seymour was a prankster who locked doors and played with light switches and the talk-listen button on the intercom that had to be disconnected. Three new intercoms had been replaced, and in the end, we could only use it for music. He enjoyed toying with you when you were alone, like the party he shared with young Ray and the TV that went on by itself when I was alone. It was not until I had a screaming fit that it finally stopped.

He was the shadow that you followed and the presence that came to comfort you when you cried—not a calming thought. And when my anger exploded, could he have seen me as a mother figure and disappeared until he recovered from hurt feelings?

I know. A mother figure to a young ghost—ridiculous, right?

CHAPTER THIRTY

Sara had just given me notice that she would be leaving. She had met someone and wanted to work closer to home. She had to take a train and three buses to get home, and she had met someone who drove the last bus. They had been dating for some time, and he had just asked her to marry him. I was very happy for Sara. But it was bittersweet. I panicked at the thought of starting over with someone else. She had been with us for the past seven years. I was spoiled, and I really liked her; it would be hard to say good-bye.

I placed an ad in the paper and advertised for live in help. A young woman called on the phone in answer to the ad. She had been a housekeeper for a gentleman who worked in the Warner Brothers film industry and had given her references. She had worked for him for two years in California, but she had come back home to Philadelphia to take care of her aunt who was ill. She had grown up with her aunt and was her only living relative. She went on to say she would take the train up from the city, and I agreed to pick her up at the train station. She told me what she would be wearing.

The next day, I pulled up to a very young and attractive woman who had answered my ad. She was tall and thin and looked more like a model than a housekeeper. She had high cheekbones, perfect white teeth, and light skin. She was dressed in a long coat that went all the way to her boots. She had a knitted hat on her head and gloves. It was winter, and snow was still on the ground from the last storm, but she was dressed for a blizzard.

I picked her up in a pickup truck, and judging from the look on her face, she had been expecting something else—maybe a limo perhaps! She started telling me about her previous employer and how she had also been their nanny. I explained to her that there were no small children as my sons were now older teenagers. I was only interested in keeping the house at its best. I explained that the house was almost three hundred years old and many times people would ask to see it. She turned her head to look at me, and I noticed she had on two knitted hats and all her hair was under them. She noticed my stare and explained that she could not get warm enough and needed to bundle up.

I would soon realize that it was so I could not identity her from the mug shots, but I am getting ahead of my story. She was taking me in as well. I had on a heavy jacket with white paint on it. There was not anything in my closet I could wear that didn't have paint on it. My hair was pulled back in a ponytail, and I don't think I was making any impressions. She started to tell me about a dinner she was going to make for the family, and I told her again that was not important to me.

I thought to myself that after a while, she'd understand what I wanted. When we got to the house, I asked her to take off her coat, and she asked politely if she could leave it on. She was still cold after coming from a warm climate.

I said, "Well, you won't need this." And as I reached for her hats, she grabbed my arm, saying that she'd like to keep it on in a tone of voice that surprised me.

We are not off to a good start, I thought. I showed her the house and, on our way back to the kitchen, asked what she thought.

She answered, "Oh, this will be easy."

It was a tone of confidence and, if I had thought about it, one of arrogance. I turned to look her in the face and said I've never heard the word *easy* used to explain housework before. She was again as sweet as she could be. She kept saying to me ever since we had pulled up to the house that I could go back to work and she would explore what needed to be done.

Not so bloody likely went through my mind.

What I did next, I would later be so happy about. I took her arm and walked her to the telephone and explained that that big white wing on the barn with all the windows looking over the house was where I worked and I could see everything from my office. I went on to say that the one button on the telephone when pushed could get me or anyone of the men who were in and out of the shop all day and that she could be assured that she would never be alone here.

She then asked if she could make herself a cup of tea to get warm. I told her I'd be back in an hour to check on her. I felt something might be wrong but still had no clue as to what it was that I was feeling. I didn't wait an hour, I walked over thirty minutes later. She was nowhere to be found. I checked in the bedroom and found my jewelry case opened. I was quite sure she was disappointed. I did not have anything expensive, only costume jewelry. But I noticed that my mother's wedding ring was gone.

My mother had given me that ring when she was on her death-bed, and I wanted it back. Each year my mother had also given me three silver dollars that had never been circulated for each of my sons. She had been doing this for my sons since they had been born.

They were also missing. I had quite a few, and I was furious.

I called the police and said I was going to look for her, but the police insisted I wait there for a squad car. They would look for her. The detectives were there even before I could look around. They found the door in the dining room was opened—only the top half. She had climbed over the bottom half of the original Dutch doors. They traced her footprints in the snow as she ran along the fence to the gates and out to the road.

"She must have had someone waiting for her outside," said the detective. "They must have followed you from the train station."

She had been in the house less than thirty minutes. She had obviously been afraid I would see her from my office (this gave me some small satisfaction), or so I thought. I was heartbroken over the few things that she did get away with.

The detective and I had just walked back into the house when another detective who had been upstairs while they were dusting for fingerprints came down the stairs. He was holding a brown handbag and asked if it was mine. I said no, but it was the one that she had been carrying. It's funny how you might not notice something from the start, but the bag she had been carrying now looked like it had been bought at a thrift shop.

He opened it up, and there was the jewelry that she had taken. My mother's ring was there, and that was all I cared about. I asked about my coins, and he said, "I have not touched this. I would like you to see it first."

He led me over to the back staircase leading from the bedroom, and there halfway down the stairs was my coin case still bulging, filled with my coins.

"It didn't even open when it was dropped," I said.

"Ma'am," said the detective, "I don't believe it was dropped. Ma'am, I think it was thrown, maybe at someone. I found the purse at the top of the steps. She dropped it there. I think she heard someone coming and didn't have any time to put the coin case in the bag, but something happened at the top of the stairs. It looks to me as if she had just put the jewelry from your case into her purse and then discovered the coins. Just then she heard someone. Maybe she thought it was you. Do you know of anyone who might have come into your house and disrupted her right in the middle of her collecting everything? I believe she threw the coin case at someone as she started down the stairs. She was really in a hurry, didn't want to spend time even opening the full dining room door. And looking at her footprints in the snow, she was running."

The other detective said, "Do you know of anyone who might have startled her back in your bedroom?"

"No, Detective, I can't think of anyone," I answered.

I turned away. A smile crossed my face, and I thought, *Was there a showdown with the shadow? What could have scared a hardcore thief?*

Whatever happened back there in my bedroom, I would never know, but later when I was alone, I whispered under my breath, "Thank you. She didn't get away with anything."

This was the first time I would think of Seymour as someone who might look out for us.

CHAPTER THIRTY-ONE

I did not want to place another ad in the paper, but I had no choice. However, if I pulled up to see someone dressed like an Eskimo, then I would keep on driving and never look back. I was never able to identify her in any mug shots. But I had great satisfaction in thinking that Seymour might have been the one who sacred her off. There could not have been any other explanation as there was no one in the house that day. I would have loved to know what happened—if he had chased her or at least she thought that he was chasing her—and why she threw that heavy coin case.

I placed an ad, and Nanina came into our lives. There were three people waiting for me at the train station that day. Her family had come with her to make sure it was a legitimate ad. She was from the Philippines. She had family here and had just come here to live and was looking for a job. She could start right away. She was a small, petite woman who liked to sing. She was always singing, and Ray joked that I would sing too if I had a job like this. She never had anyone bother her, and she kept the house the way I wanted it. She was very nice to have around. I had no intentions of ever telling her about Seymour.

Everyone in our house knew not to say a word. She spoke broken English, but I suspected she was very smart and articulate. She showed me a letter she was writing to her niece. She could spell better than me and wrote beautifully. After only a week, I knew she was staying. I liked her a lot, and I think she felt the same. She had not mentioned anything unusual, and just when I was getting to think *he* was away, it happened.

I had just come in the back door, carrying groceries, when Nanina came down the kitchen steps and asked me if I wanted help.

"That would be great, thank you," I said.

"How you do that?" she asked in her broken English.

I answered, "Do what?"

She said, "Call me, and then you walk in! I heard you calling me upstairs, but you were just coming in when I walked into the kitchen. How you do that?"

I stood there for a second and thought for a minute then proceeded to tell her that sometimes strange things happened in the house that could not be explained. I should have been looking at her face when I said this, but I wasn't, and I continued on to say that we have a ghost living in our house!

I heard a noise, and as I turned around, I was just in time to grab her arm as her legs buckled and she went to the floor. Her other hand was grasping her cross that she wore around her neck. She was praying in her native tongue. What was I thinking?

I never use that word. How could I have been that stupid? These things had to be handled delicately. You might have thought that I had just mentioned demons or the devil. I had to think fast, or I was about to lose a good housekeeper.

"Oh, Nanina, I am so sorry. I was only kidding. I didn't mean to scare you. I was joking, really."

It took a minute for her to stop praying, open her eyes, and look at me. I was desperate. I would deal with this later, but right then, I lied.

"Nanina, we don't have ghosts. Who would want to live here? No one! I did not know that my kidding you would make you so nervous. I am sorry. I will never do that again."

The color started to return to her face as I helped her to a chair.

"I am not sure what you heard, but I am glad you came downstairs to help me. Just sit there a minute and get your breath. I'll put these bags away."

She did not say a word. I went on talking about the traffic that time of year—it was the fall—and how things were getting busy.

Then she said in a quiet voice that she could not live in a house that was possessed.

"Of course not," I gasped, "neither could I."

The days went by, and I waited for the next shoe to drop, but nothing happened. I could not believe it. Nanina said nothing about anything unusual. She was with us for the next four years, and nothing was ever said again. I think this is a fine illustration of how someone can live in a haunted house and not see it. Oh, I don't mean see a ghost but choose to ignore strange events and accept them as normal. I was quite sure he still closed or opened doors or, on occasion, locked the bathroom door and perhaps wrinkled the bed covers. But whatever happened or didn't, she accepted it and reasoned it away, the same way I did in our early years.

I could never believe that Seymour went easy on her, but I never brought up the subject again, so I will never know. It was the same way with Ray Sr. We had for years lived here, and I still don't know what Ray believes. I think he was content not to think about any of it.

But he, Seymour, still did his things to let us know he was there.

CHAPTER THIRTY-TWO

⁂

Our boys were in serious relationships now. Ray Jr. was seeing Lisa, and they were talking about getting married. They were even talking about buying a house together. They had never mentioned to me that Lisa had had an encounter once with Seymour. It was years earlier, shortly after they had first met. They had been dating for the past five years. I learned about this over dinner one night.

We invited the two of them out to dinner, and it was during the evening that the talk turned to Seymour. It happened the night they were going to a concert. Ray was in our bathroom, and Lisa was watching him in the mirror standing behind young Ray.

He was using his dad's best cologne. He watched Lisa in the mirror as she turned and walked away. Something in the mirror behind her had caught her eye, and she turned around to see a shadow move just past the door and out of sight. She walked out into our dressing room and was surprised to see a young boy about thirteen or fourteen years old walking ahead of her. She followed him out of our bedroom and into the hallway leading to Mark and Mike's bedroom. He stopped, and when he looked back at her, a boyish smile crossed his face just before he disappeared into Mike and Mark's bedroom.

In all the years we had lived there, thirteen years to date, no one had ever seen him. This was the first time we were hearing about this. I know it sounds strange that these things might happen and no one wants to tell everyone. You take these events in stride once you have accepted that there is someone else that shares this home with you. Then it becomes ordinary. Of course, it was not for Lisa. Maybe *disbelief* is a better word. You doubt your eyes at first. But I can assure you, you do get used to these things and don't associate these events with fear—not anymore.

It's more an aha moment that you were allowed to see this, a window to the past, and that he shared this moment with you. She shared her story with us, which lasted only a few minutes. She said he was dressed like you would expect to see a boy in the seventieth century. He was wearing short pants that were just below the knee. She did not notice the shoes, but she described him as wearing a white blouse with long sleeves and that he wore his tousled hair long over his ears and to his neck, though it was short with bangs. When he smiled, it was sweet—no malice, just like you would expect if you were meeting a young boy for the first time. He was handsome!

Now I knew he was a young boy, and I was quite sure his name was Derrick. I was sure now that he was the young boy who died at age thirteen years and six weeks, as stated in the records. And I now believe he was the only entity who lived here, except for the gentleman who smoked his pipe in the dining room. Of course, even thirteen-year-olds might emulate their fathers who smoked a pipe. I wondered, *Does anyone else have stories that I had not heard about? And could he be the only soul who lives here?*

Mark's girlfriend was Michele, and yes, I was sure that our sons had told their girlfriends about the stories that they had grown up with and the many things that had happened to them. But this was very different from what anyone had ever seen, and he chose to show himself to Lisa. I had no doubt of this. This also had happened long before I had done any research and had suspected it might be a young boy.

I saw Michele the next day. I had hired her to work in the office of our company as I knew one day she too would be my daughter-in-law as well as Lisa. I waited for a moment when we could talk without interruption. We all lived busy lives, and that often accounted for why we never get to hear about things that might have happened to our children. We were eating lunch in the kitchen, just the two of us, when I asked her if anything had ever happened to her when she was in the house.

She helped me with filing and answering the phones. At first, she answered this question with no. She had heard all the stories, but as she went on to talk, she said with some hesitation that the only time something had happened was when she had gone up in the TV room to watch her soap opera show. It was her favorite that came on at noon.

She had not told me about this, because she felt funny watching her soap opera during her lunch break. I assured her it was okay since it was her lunch break, and she continued on to say that after she had watched her show, she got up to leave the room. She turned off the TV, but it came on again. She explained that she thought maybe she had not held the switch all the way down and that was why it had gone on again. So she took the remote and held the button until the TV had disappeared into the box. Then she laid the remote on the coffee table, but as she moved to walk out of the room, the TV came on again.

I asked what she did then, and she answered in a high-pitched voice, "Nothing! I went out of the house as fast as I could."

I had never told any of my kids about the events with the TV when it happened to me as it was still in the early years and I did not want to add to their imagination or instill any idea of any ghost. I smiled when Michele finished telling me her story but did not tell her that it had happened to me.

There are a great many things that I have written on these pages that my children will be reading for the first time. I've always wondered if there are more stories that I have never heard from my children. We have lived here for thirteen years, and this was the first time I had heard Lisa's story or Michele's. I am sure Seymour has been doing his thing for a couple of hundred years and we are not the only ones who have felt his presence or endured his pranks.

I had wanted to live here for the rest of my life, but with my sons talking about getting married, my husband was already crying that the farm would be too much work for the two of us to keep up without their help. I would not listen when he would start talking about putting the farm up for sale, but in my heart, I knew it was an era that was soon coming to an end.

CHAPTER THIRTY-THREE

O ne night, Ray and I had just returned from having dinner when I walked into the kitchen to find a puppy in the center of our three dogs. I quickly called out to my sons, and to my surprise, no one was home. I was quite sure that one of my sons had dropped off this dog and left. Ray was already giving me a hard time.

He was already saying, "Whatever their story is, the dog has to go."

"Why are you raising your voice?" I asked.

"Because I know you!" he answered.

"Oh, look," I said. It looks like Tara has already adopted him." She had wrapped herself around him and was licking his face, just like a mom would do when mothering her puppy.

Ray left the room in a huff. He knew he never won these fights. But this time, I understood his frustration. We had been talking about downsizing—at least Ray had.

If we were to keep collecting animals, it would require a home the size of what we had.

The whole idea of moving was to go smaller. But Tara and the pup were so cute together.

Just then, Mark came home. He started talking the moment he walked through the door.

"Before you say anything, Mom, you need to hear me out." Mark went on to say that he and Michele had gone shopping at the mall. When they went outside and walked to the car, this puppy, was running in between the parked cars. "He came to me, and I bent down and reached out my hand. He was scared and hungry.

So I slowly walked around him and picked him up. I looked around the parking lot to see if anyone was looking for him, but I didn't see anyone."

"Well, I am glad your father has already gone upstairs. You know he would have had a fit. You would have been taking your pup to Michele's house. Tomorrow, we'll run an ad in the paper to see if anyone is looking for him.

"Mom, what was I to do? I couldn't just leave him there."

"No," I answered, "of course not. I would have done the same." I watched as a look of relief came over his face.

The next morning, I read him the ad that I was placing in the paper: "Lost dog found in parking lot of Neshaminy mall, running around parked cars. Looks to be a Border collie type, black, tan with a white strip going down his face. About fifteen pounds. Please call this number."

I looked at Mark, and he was struggling to say something.

"What's wrong?" I asked.

"That's not quite what happened."

"Oh, Mark, the only way I calmed your dad down was by telling him that we could find his owner."

"Well, the part that we were shopping is true. But we were at the I-75 mart, where they sell a lot of animals to anyone. I was telling this man he could not keep five dogs in one crate together. They were lying on top of one another and could not even stand up. He opened up the crate and said, 'If you're so upset, then buy him and there'll be more room for the others.' He held him up by the back of his neck, and the poor thing just hung there. I thought he might be dead. Mom, you've got to do something."

I have been involved in animal welfare for many years, but knew he was still diverting the issue. "Let's stay with the story first. What am I going to tell your dad?"

"We are thinking about moving, and we are still getting more animals. Mom, neither one of you would have walked away from this."

I told Mark that when I went to touch the back of the pup's neck for a rub, he had cried. But when I walked away from him, he barked. He had a lot of spunk for a little dog as I believed he was telling me off.

"I will have to tell your dad that if we can't find his owner, then we will look for a good home."

Mark smiled.

Who was I kidding? I really like the little guy, and after hearing his story, I knew the best home for him was here with us.

"What shall we call him?" I asked.

Mark answered, "Michele and I have already given him a name. We like Duke."

CHAPTER THIRTY-FOUR

R ay was not giving up about moving. He knew I did not want to leave my farm, but he talked me into meeting with a realtor just to see what it would sell for. I believe the words he used were "to test the waters." He said it would be nice to see what all our hard work was now worth.

The following week, we invited a realtor over to show off the farm. We sat in the kitchen after having given her the tour in much the same way we had been given the tour thirteen years ago. When she told us what she would list it for, I watched Ray's face light up. You would have thought that he had just been given the jackpot from a winning lottery ticket. I knew I was doomed.

Once he told the kids, they too would want to sell. We had promised the boys that we would give them enough money they could put down on a house. And they really deserved it. They had earned every penny. But I was not willing to give up. I had Seymour.

The realtor was telling us about the paperwork that she and her office would take care of, and as she turned a blank agreement of sale to show us, there was a loud sound just behind us. We even ducked our heads as the sound of crashing glass flew across the floor and into the kitchen. There was a trail of shattered glass that led from the kitchen to the dining room. As we walked into the dining room, the glass crunched under our feet. A glass print that had hung in the dining room was in shambles. It was so badly damaged it appeared it had been slammed against the floor.

Ray and I knew who did it, and we had a pretty good idea why. We looked back into the kitchen, and the realtor was still sitting at the table, acting like things get smashed around her all the time. She was writing, and I believe she was filling out the agreement. This is why things can happen and people just suppose it's normal. We assured her we were not ready to sign just now but would talk about it and let her know. She never said a word about what had just happened.

When she left, we went back into the dining room to clean up the damage. We checked the hook that the picture had been hanging on for years. It came as no surprise to us when we saw that the picture had not slipped off the hook, nor did the hook pull out of the wall. No, it was still intact and as solid in the wall as the first day it had been nailed there. The picture could only have been picked up off the hook and then thrown down in rage to have spread that much glass across the floor and left the frame in many broken pieces.

This was a first. He had never shown us any anger—never. I asked Ray what he believed had just happened and if he thought Seymour might be upset. Ray only smiled and shook his head back and forth. That's as much as I ever got from Ray.

I concluded that Seymour thought we had sold the house and was upset. I still wanted to talk to more realtors, and I settled on one realtor who had agreed to list the farm at a great deal more money. Ray said with anger that I had done this so as to price the farm too high. I was satisfied. The first people to look at the farm were antique dealers and needed the large barn. They had two showings but, in the end, settled on another home. That was close. I told Ray he had only the three months on the listing agreement, and then we agreed not to list again.

Of course, the boys were on their dad's side. All the animals were going with us, even the cats and horses, or he would never get my signature on a contract. That was probably why Ray had agreed to keep the farm as, in the end, we'd still need another barn. Everything here was already finished.

I was working in the company when the realtor came through with a doctor and his wife. I never dreamed a doctor would want all this work. We still needed five mowers going in the summer, and in the winter, the horses were in every night and all the time when it snowed. It was full-time work. It just never occurred to me that they might not even care about the barn and have no animals to take care of. That was exactly what happened.

They fell in love with the house. When they made another appointment, I made sure I was there. After all, they would need to be told what they might expect if they wanted to live here. They were introduced to me, and then Ray, while still holding my arm, told the realtors to do their own tour with their clients. Everyone seemed to be on the same page—keep the potential buyers away from me.

That's okay, I thought.

I had time on my side, and I had Seymour.

One day the realtor called and said they wanted to come through again and that they, the doctor and his wife, wanted to make an offer. I chuckled at the thought. An offer wasn't going to do it. I smiled to myself. I felt so smug. Only one month to go, and the farm would be off the market. Ray was out on an estimate, and I was the only one here that day and the one they would have to deal with. I chuckled with the ideas of what I could come up with.

Should I play Seymour up as evil? Or perhaps he, Seymour, could help me out with some kind of demonstration? As the couple was winding down their tour, our realtor asked if they could ask me some questions. I'd be happy to answer any questions.

I had a grin you might see on a cat while the mouse inched closer—or is it the spider to the fly? Whichever. I was about to give my greatest performance.

They wanted to know what our electric bills were, and I answered, "Oh, it's not the electric bills you have to worry about." "It's the ghosts. You do believe in ghosts, don't you?"

The doctor's realtor spun her clients around. The realtor was gasping for breath saying she had forgotten the time and had to leave immediately to meet someone at her home. At this point, I realized she was the one giving that great performance. Our realtor had, at the same time, spun me around on my heel, saying he too had not noticed the time and had to go. He looked over my shoulder, saying to the couple that he would meet them at his office as their realtor pushed them out the door.

They had done this so well together that it had to have been orchestrated before; it had been executed at the exact moment of my question. Did the couple even have time to think about what I had just said? I now knew that they were all aware that I did not want to give up my farm, and they must have been told I was capable of saying anything. This was going to be harder than I thought. And where was Seymour all this time? If ever I needed him, it was now.

The realtor called us a few days later. I had not told Ray anything about what I had said or had happened. They were all coming back again.

Ray asked the realtor, "How many times are the couple going to tour the house?"

The realtor told Ray that he was bringing with them a signed agreement of sale and added it was a very good offer. It was then that Ray told me that they did not want me there. I was insulted, but it was okay because he had mentioned *offer* and we all knew I didn't do offers.

But I would leave that for Ray to tell them. I had agreed to wait in the cottage. They had just finished when Ray brought the agreement of sale down for me to look at. They had offered us $25,000 under the full asking price. And anyone would have agreed it was a good offer, if you really wanted to sell. I was surprised that Ray did not give me a hard time when I refused to accept. We both agreed it would be full price or nothing. I must say I was shocked when all the cars drove out of the driveway without saying a word or even a good-bye. I really felt bad for Ray, but I really don't think in the end he was ready to sell.

We were content that we had had an offer that matched our dreams, but the dream we were living in was still better. Of course, our sons were not talking to us. They were sure we had blown the opportunity of a lifetime.

Four days later, in the early morning, Ray answered the phone. It was the realtor, our realtor, and he had been sitting on a signed agreement of sale for a full-price offer, but he was waiting to see if we were finished playing games.

When they had all left four days ago, they had gone back to the office and drawn up a new agreement for the full purchase price. The realtor had a signed agreement. He started to tell Ray that his office had the right to sue for their full commission if we did not accept this agreement. I heard Ray tell the realtor that we were ready to sell. My heart dropped.

The realtor for the doctor was the first to arrive. I was walking across the driveway, and as she walked towards me, I started to cry. She walked over, put her arms around me, and also started to cry.

I looked at her between sobs and asked, "I know why I am crying, but why are you?"

She answered, "My son left for college today, and I am very emotional."

We both shared a laugh.

The agreement called for inspections, and I thought, *Good. I have another chance to tell them about Seymour.*

When I finally did have a chance to tell them that they were buying a house that had a ghost living here, both the doctor and his wife smiled as if I had made it all up as a last attempt to derail the sale of my home. Of course, the realtors didn't help; in that moment, they both laughed and shuttled them out the door, saying they'd be in touch with all the details of settlement. I lost all hope after that.

I did not know then that I had already heard the last from Seymour.

When he smashed the picture in the dining room while we interviewed the first realtor, he had said his good-bye. That was the last time I would ever hear from Seymour.

* * * * *

I hear the voice of my husband leading everyone down the back staircase. I am still here, standing alone in my living room for the very last time. And I am filled with remorse.

"I will miss you, Seymour," I whispered. "I now know that there is life after death. I have learned that from you. When my time comes to cross over, if allowed, I'll come back here to see you again once more to say with love, 'It's time to say good night, Seymour.'"

153

ABOUT THE AUTHOR

Roberta Trail is retired from her business of home furnishings and design. *Say Good Night, Seymour* is her first book. She lives in Florida with her husband, Ray, and their dog, Sadie. She has eight grandchildren and two great-grandchildren. Roberta has always been a passionate advocate for the welfare of animals and children.

www.ingramcontent.com/pod-product-compliance
Lightning Source LLC
Chambersburg PA
CBHW041258040426
42334CB00028BA/3065